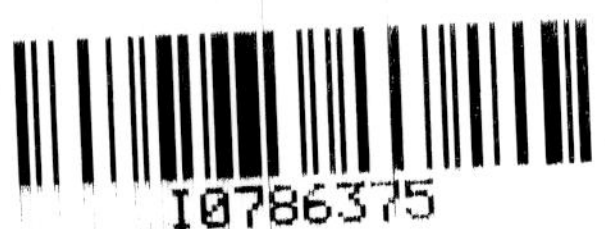

Calming
Coloring Books

Copyright: Published in the United States by Peter Raymond
Published July 2018
ISBN-13: 978-1722287764
ISBN-10: 1722287764

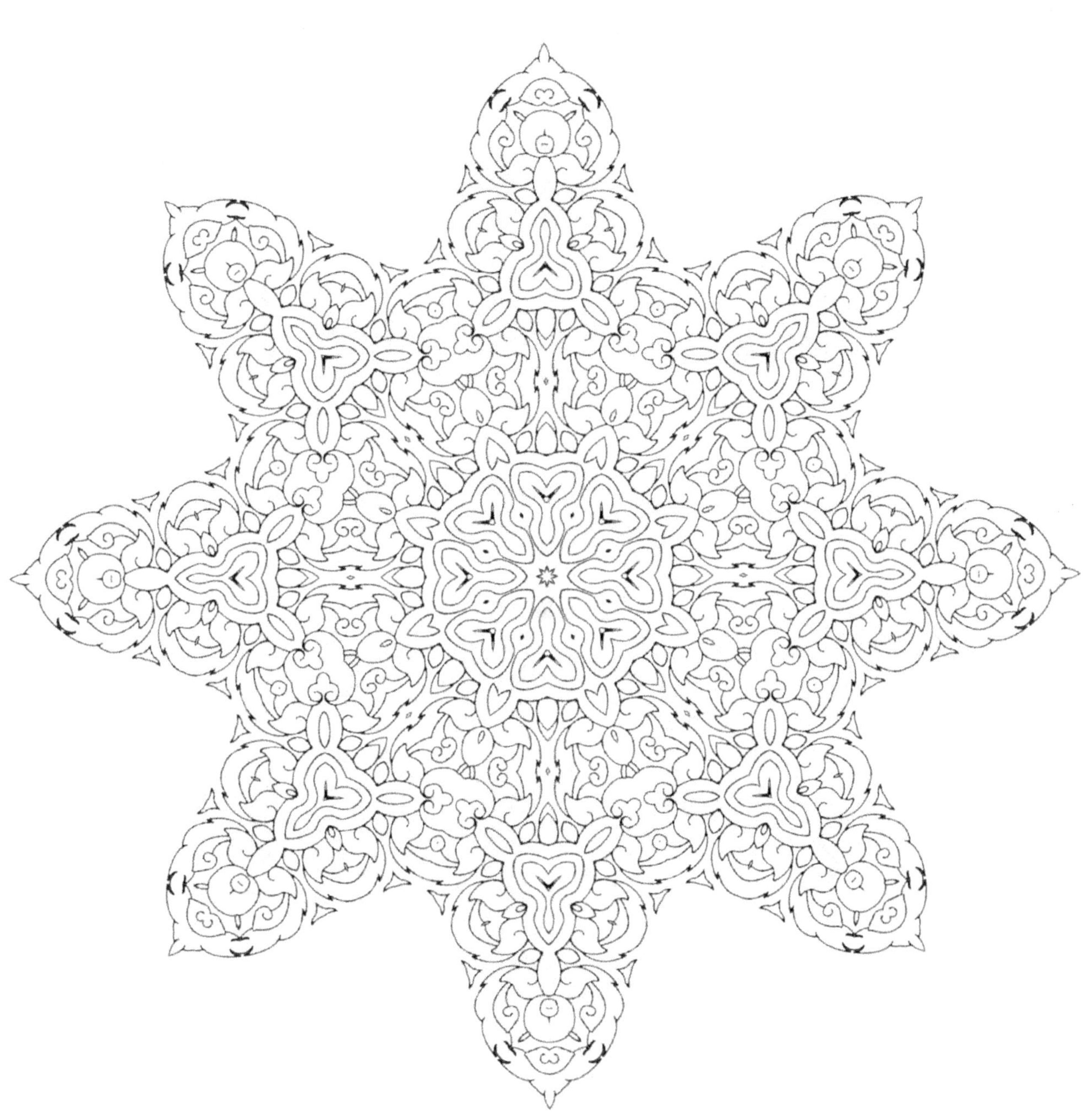

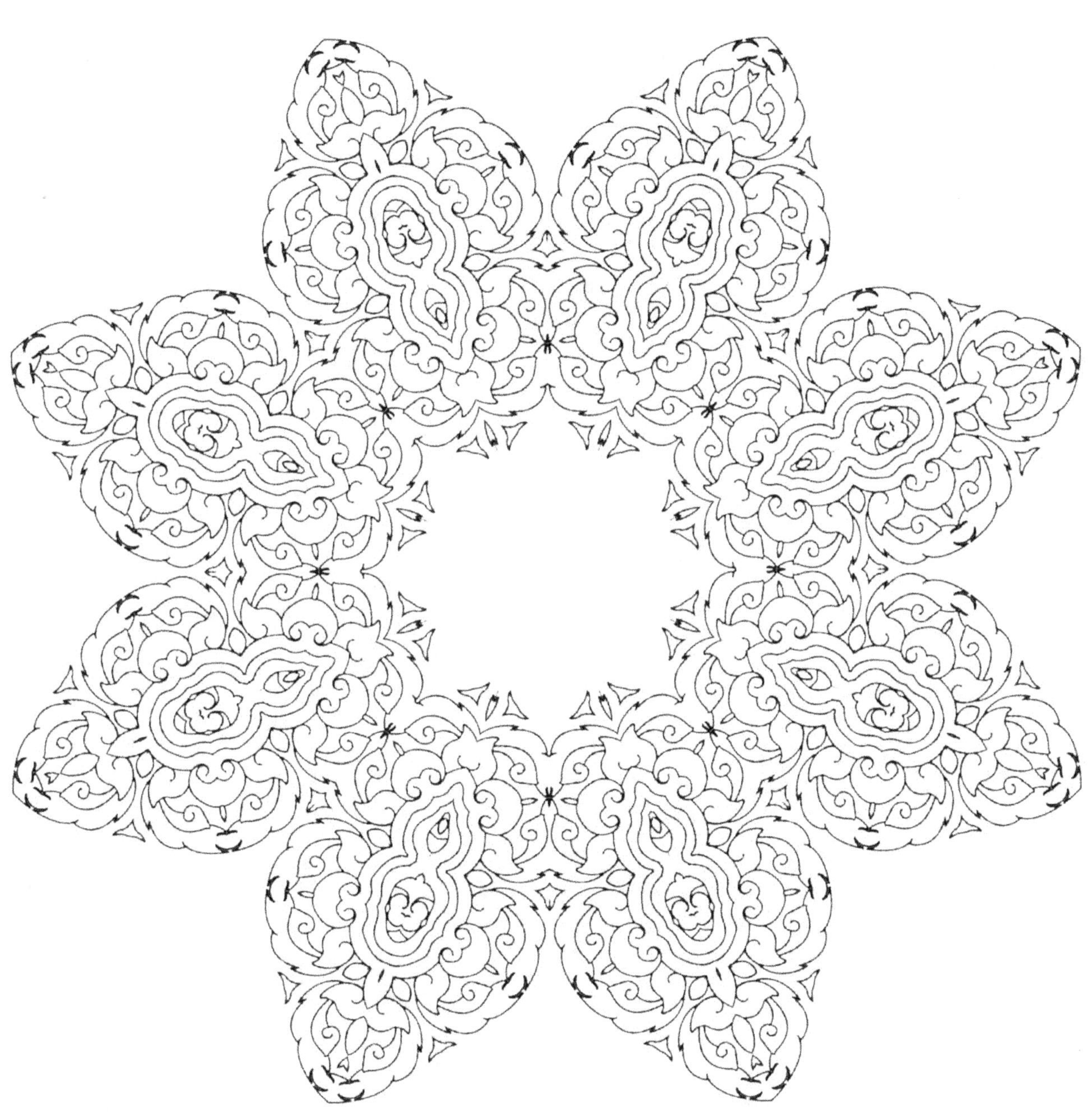

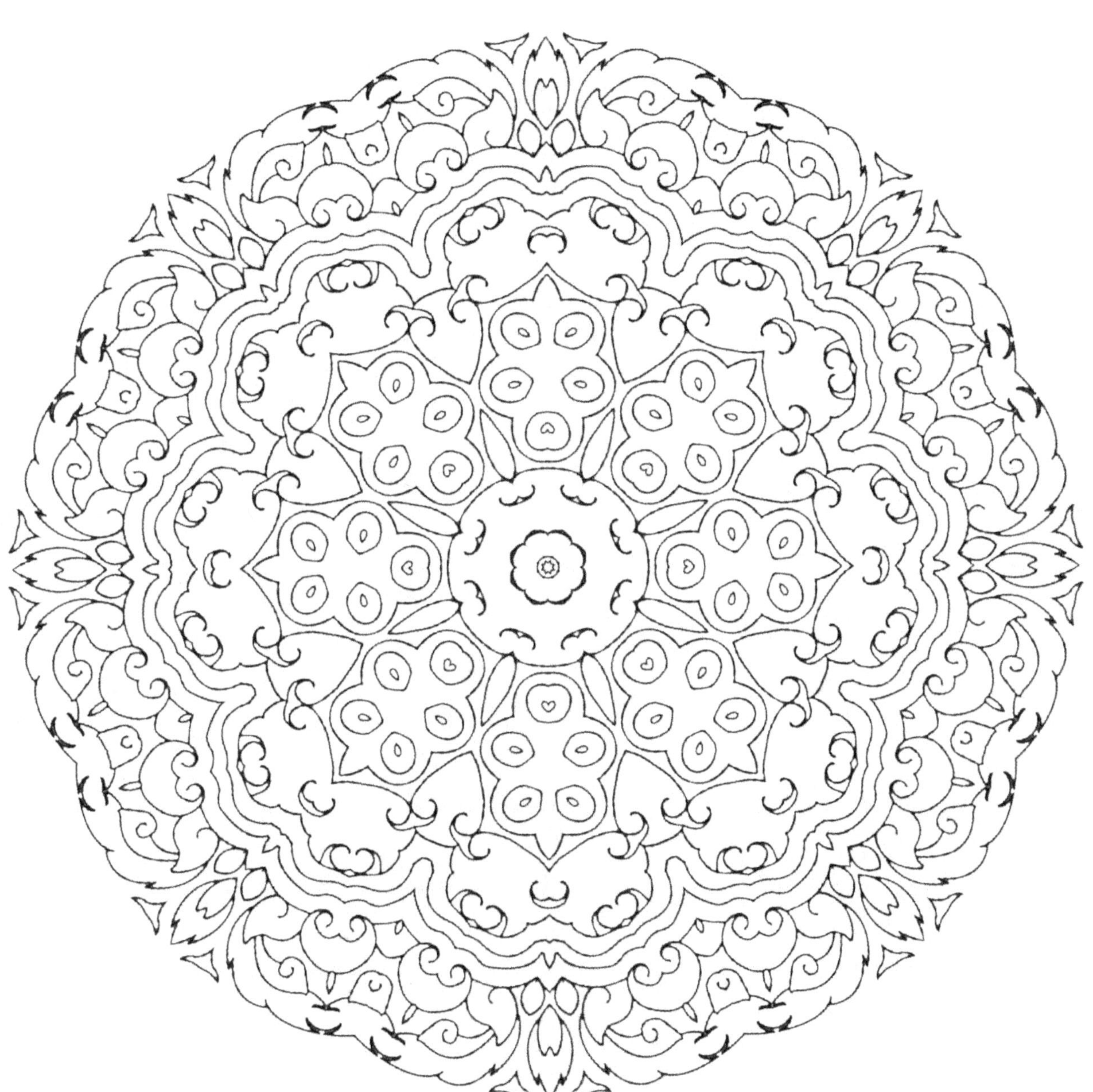

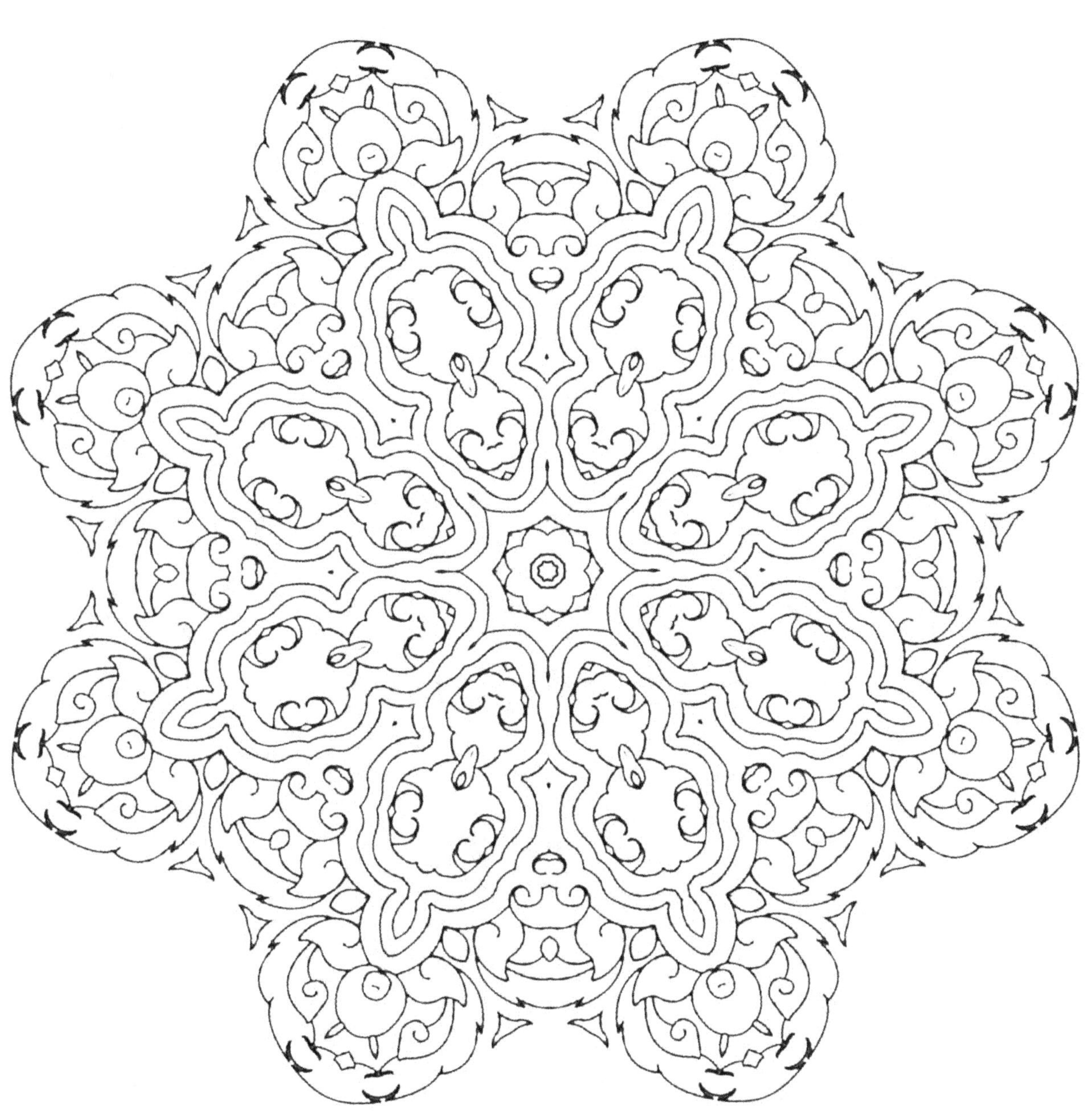

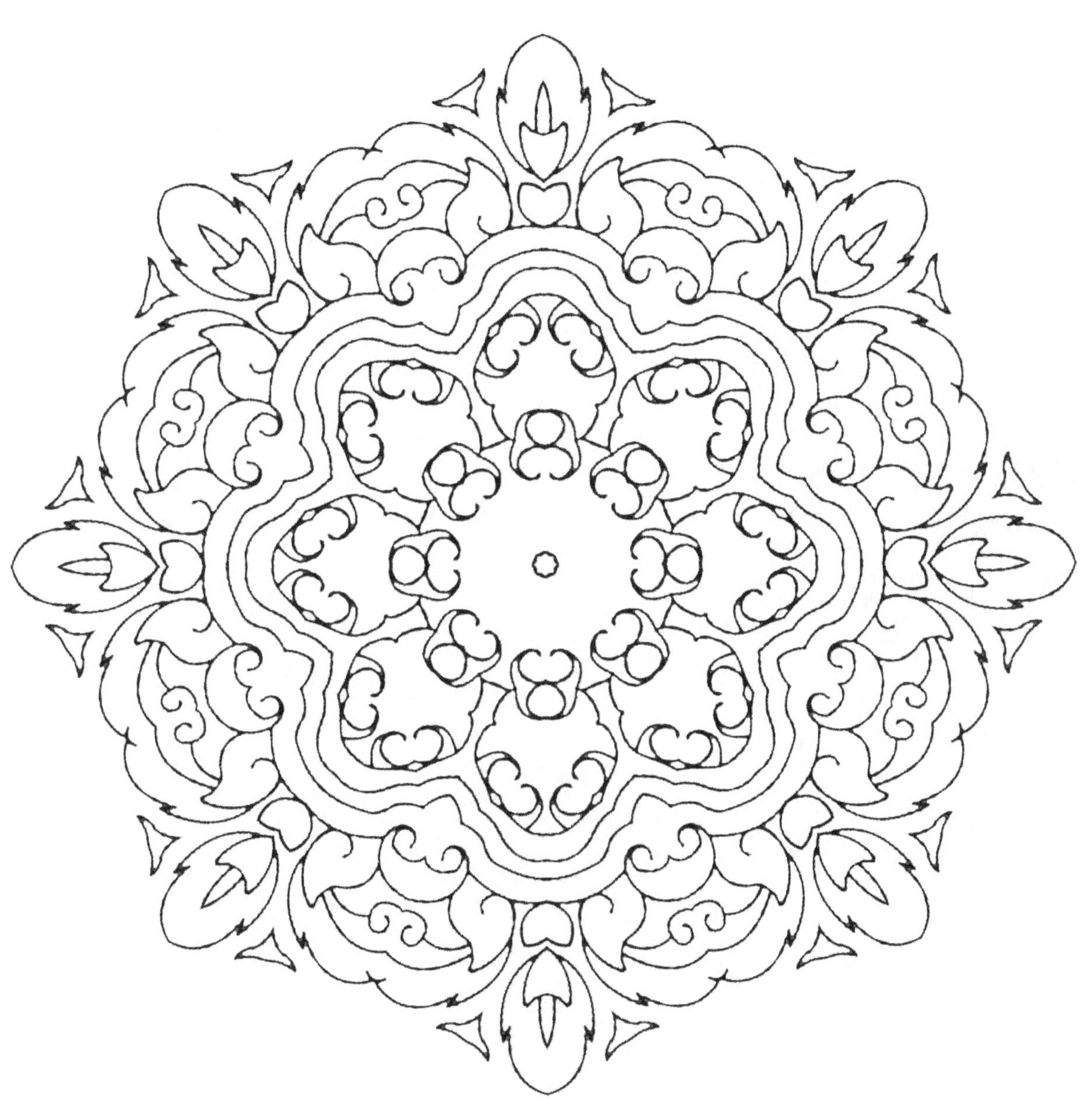

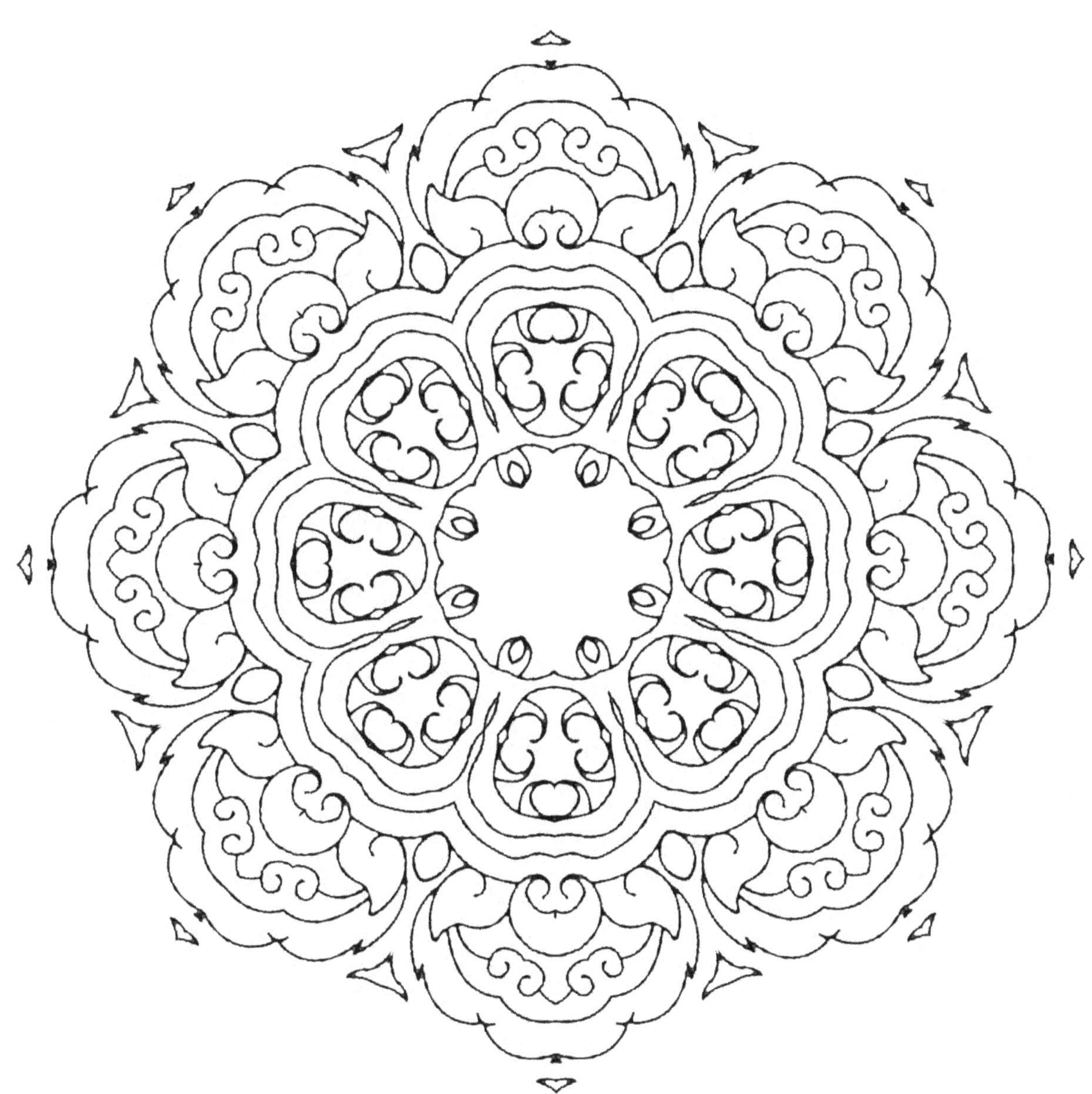

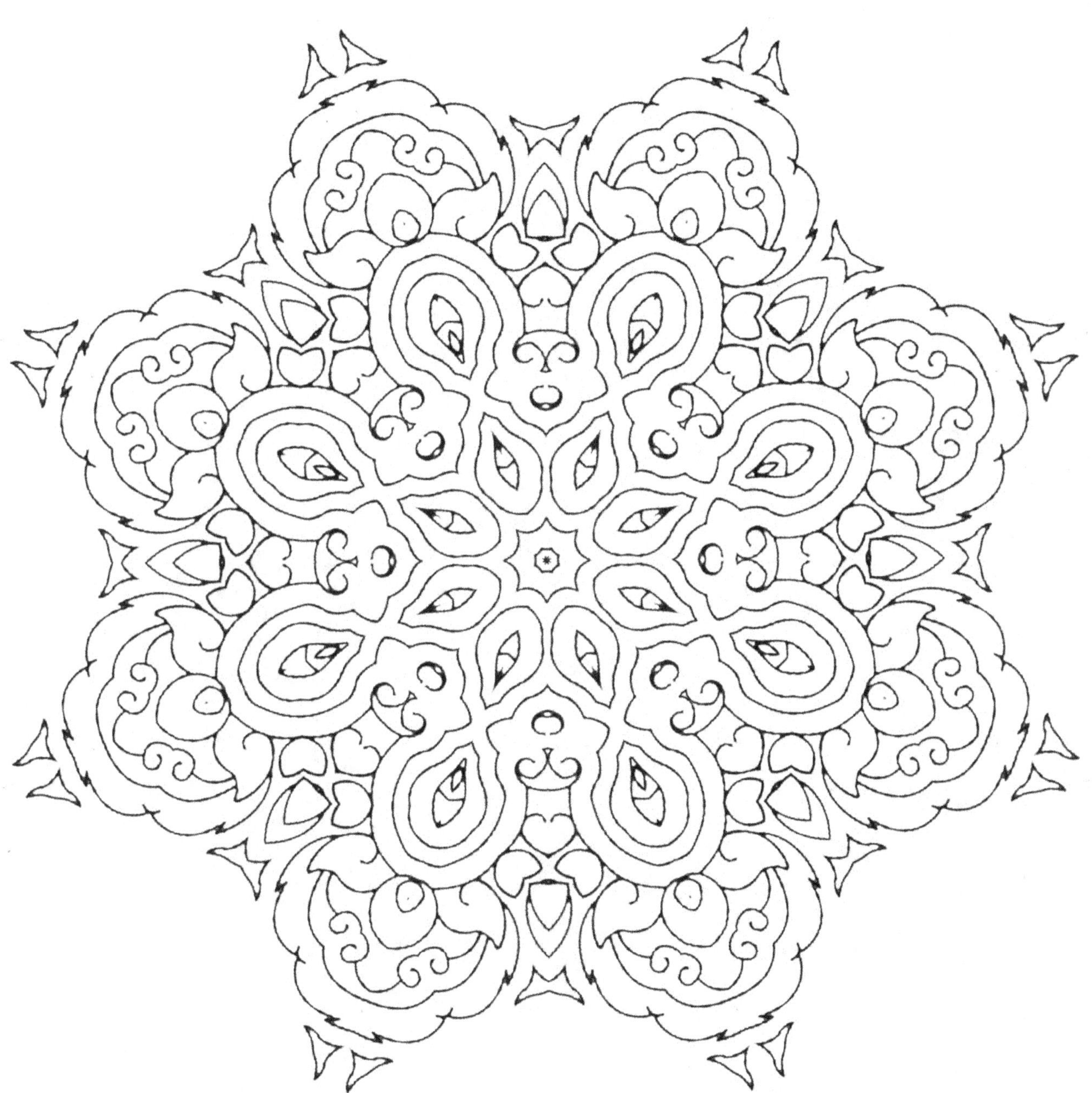

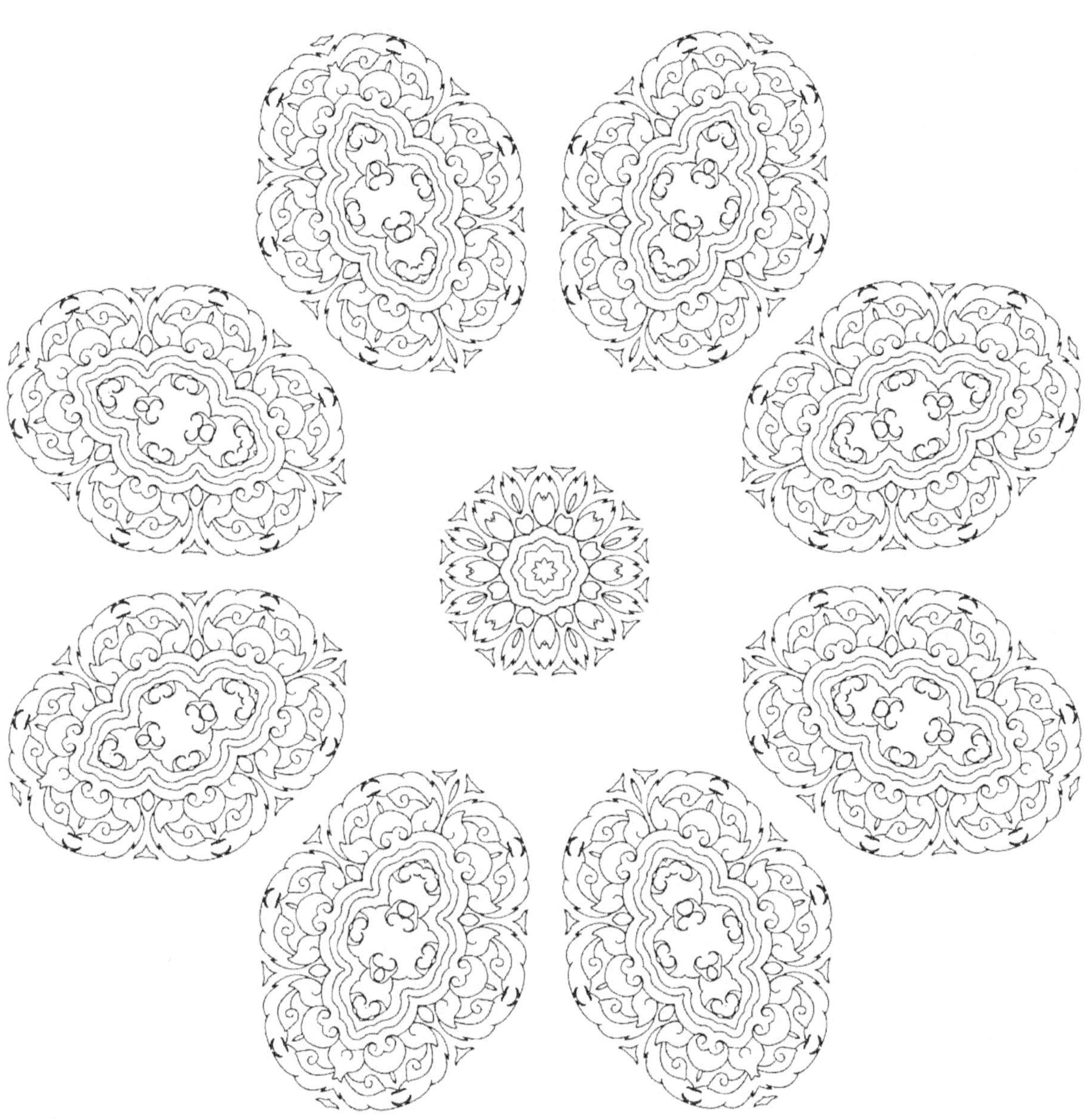

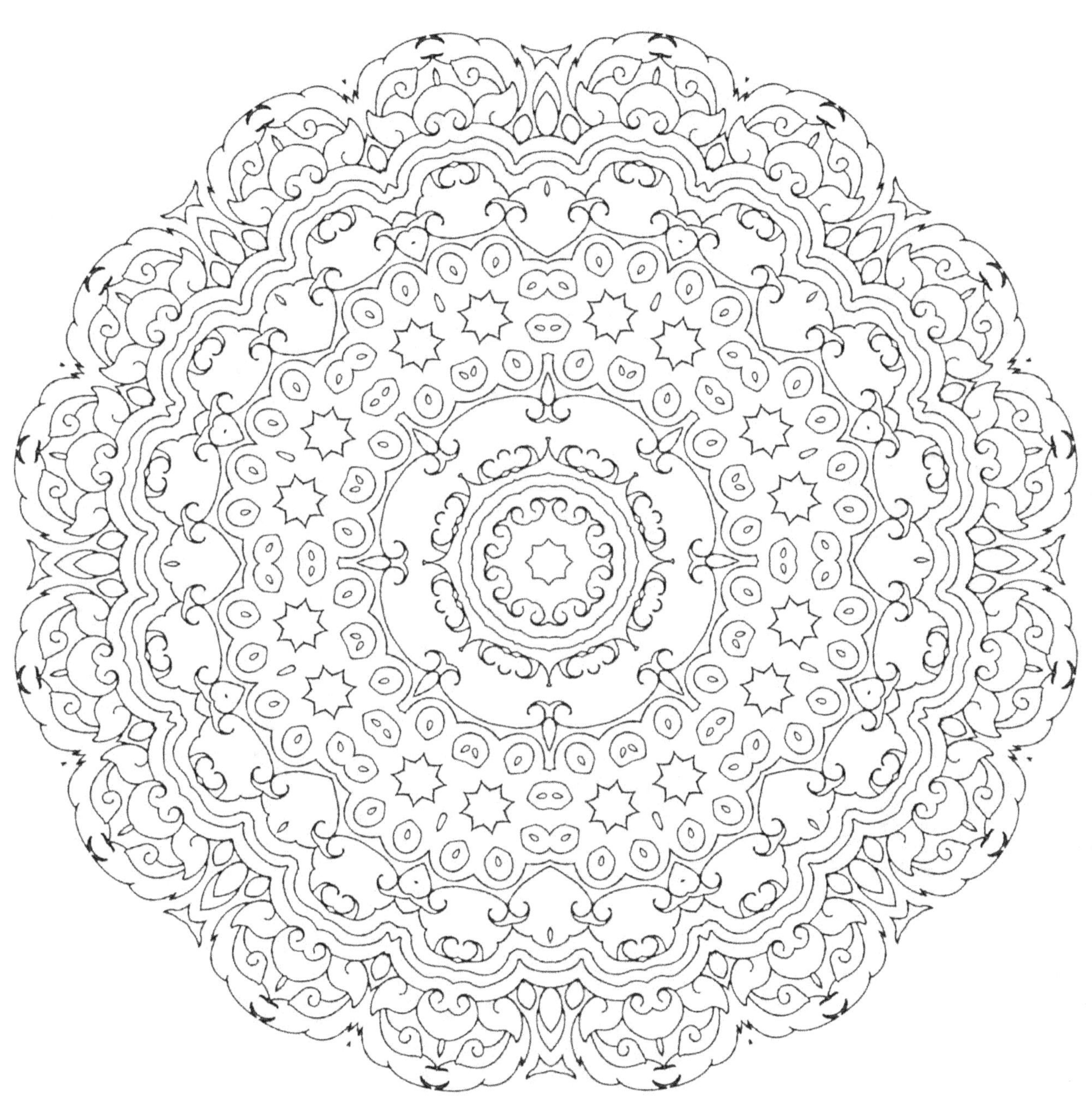

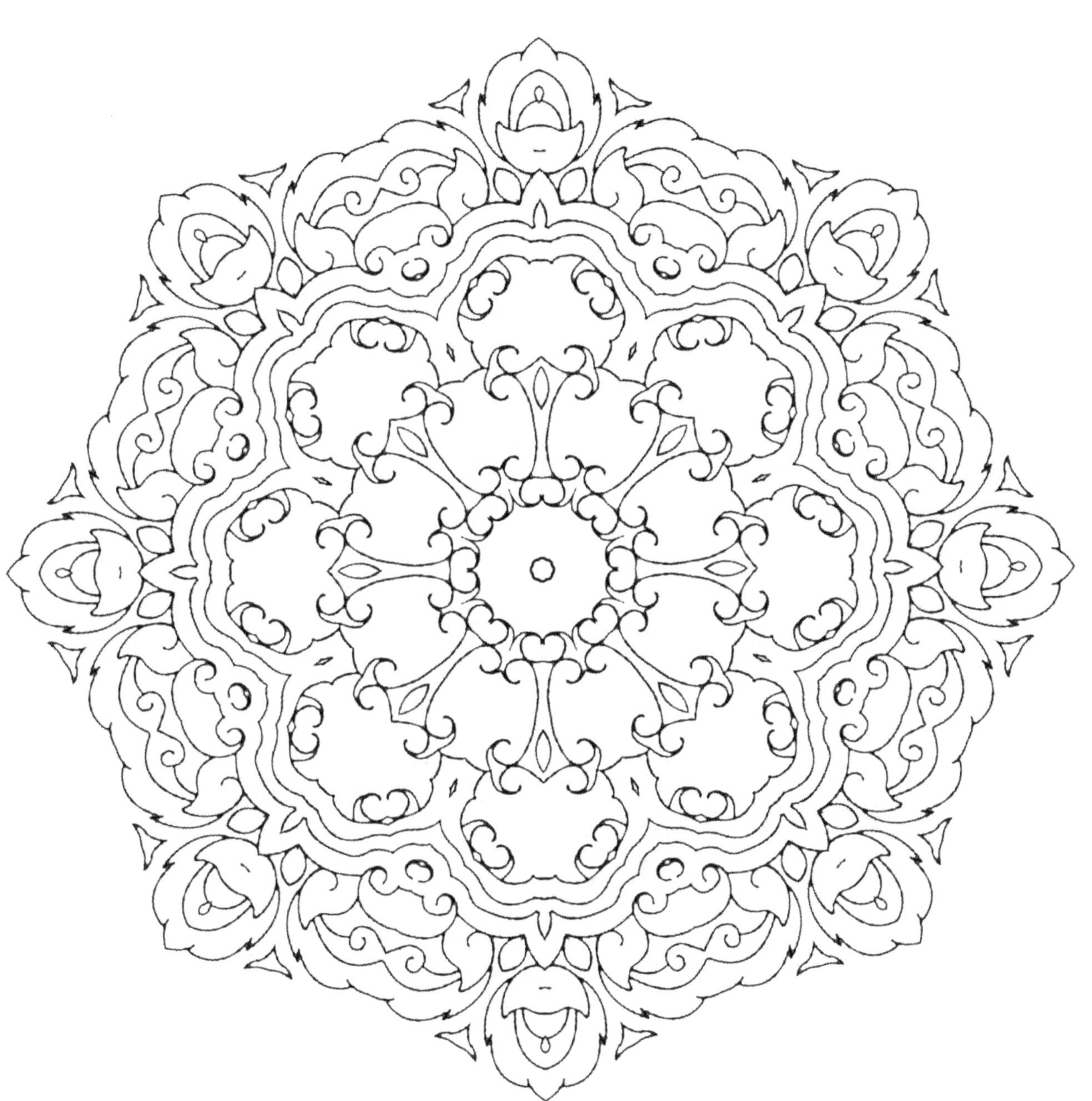

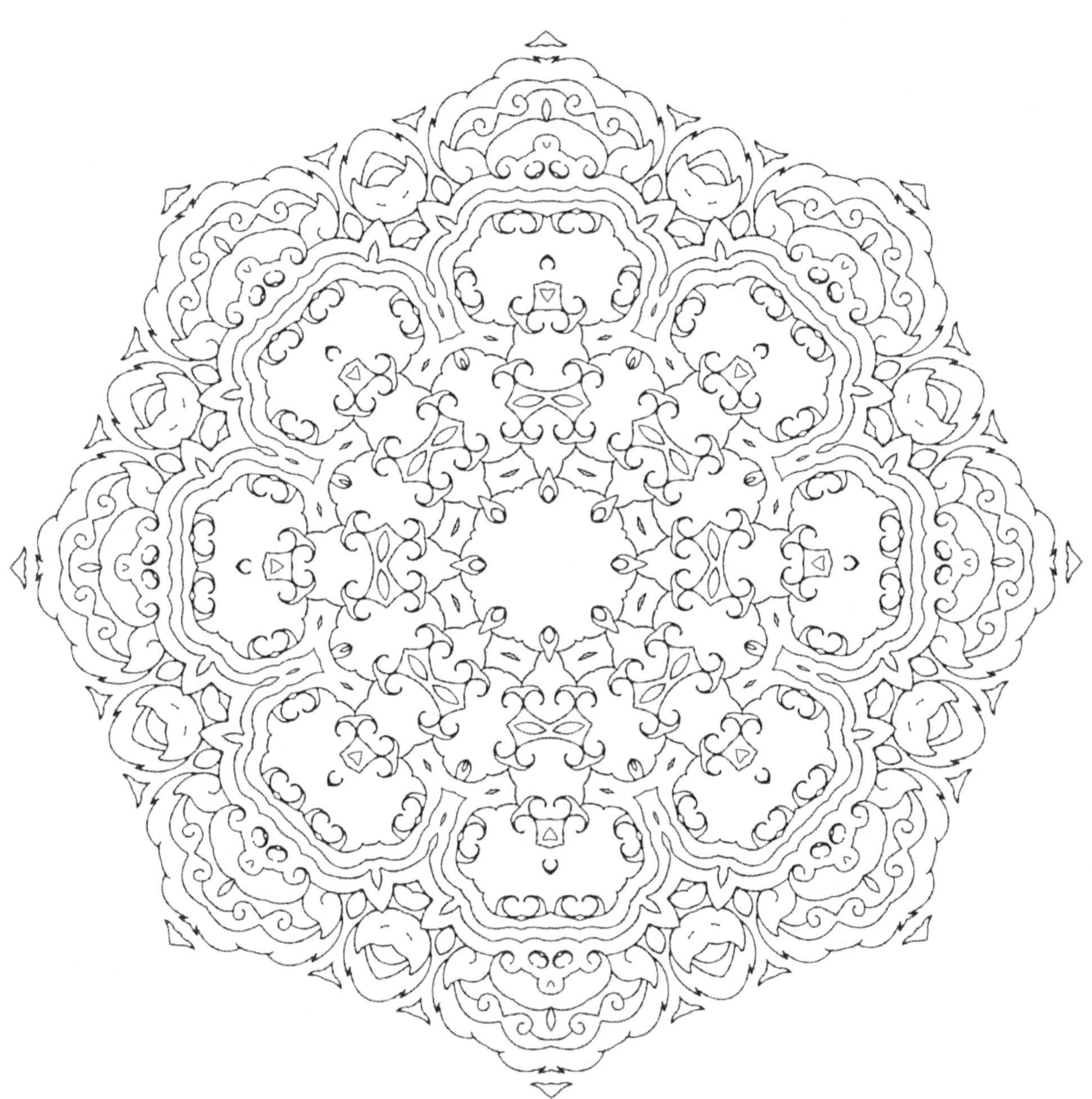

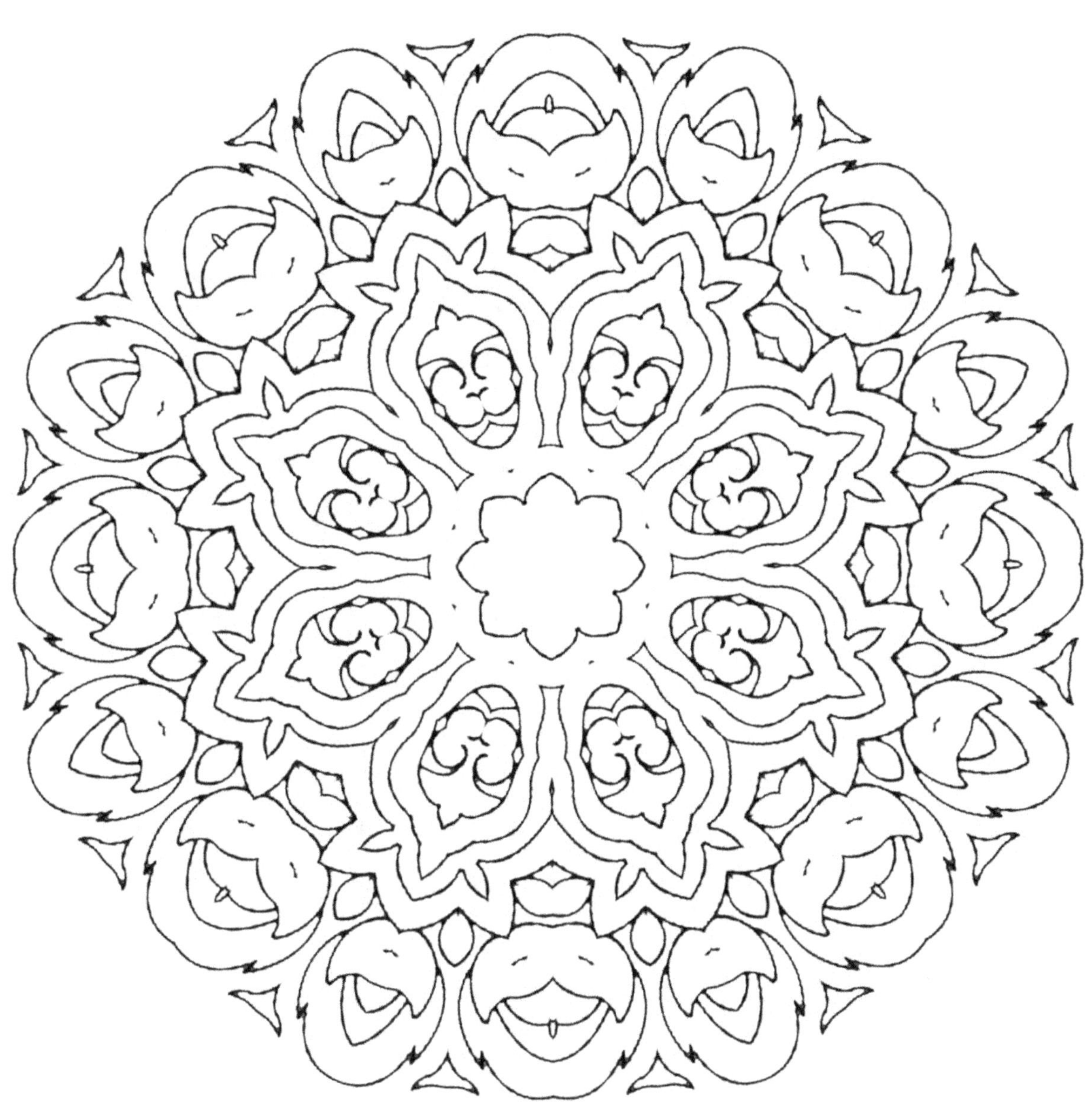

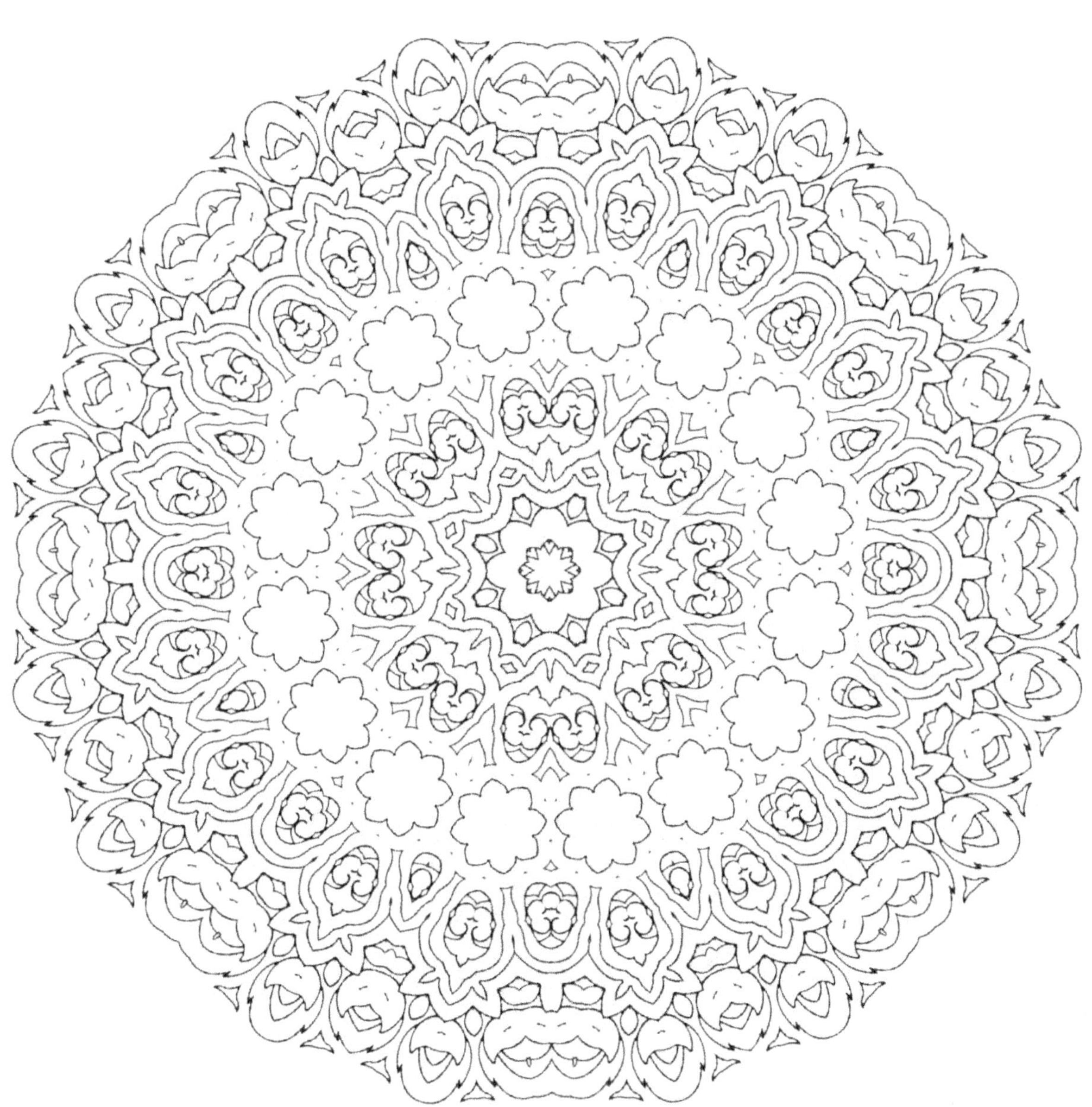

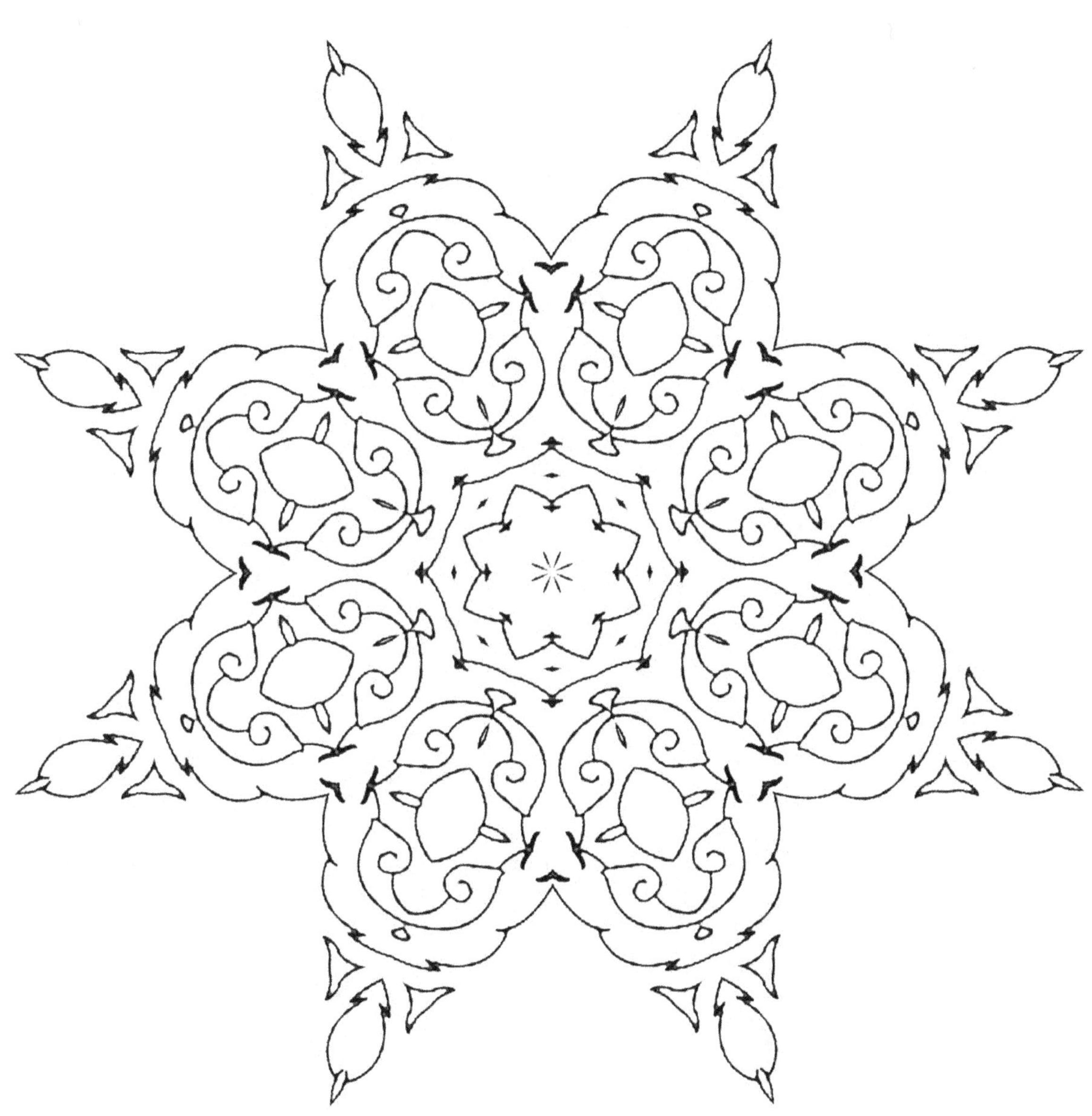

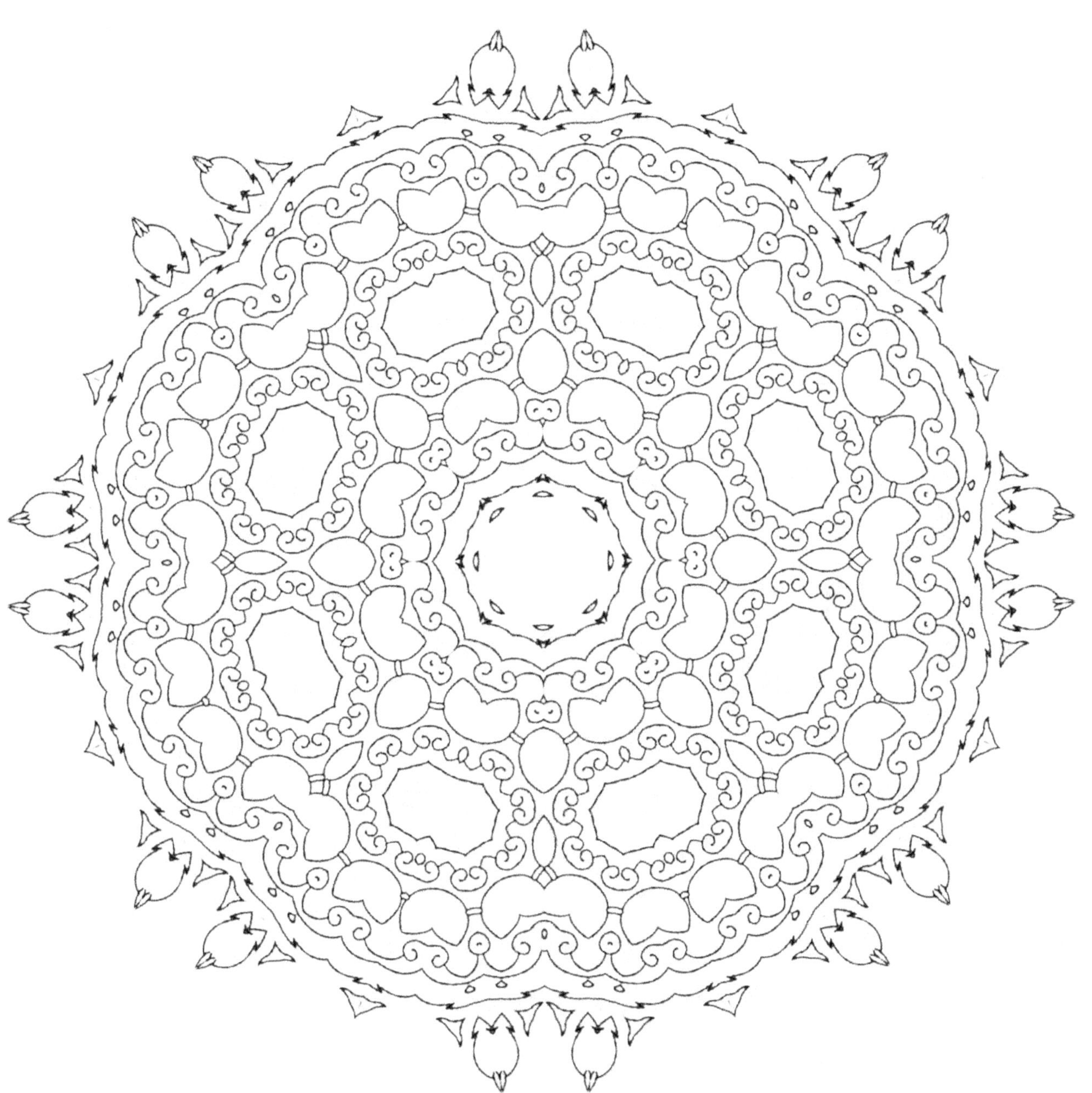

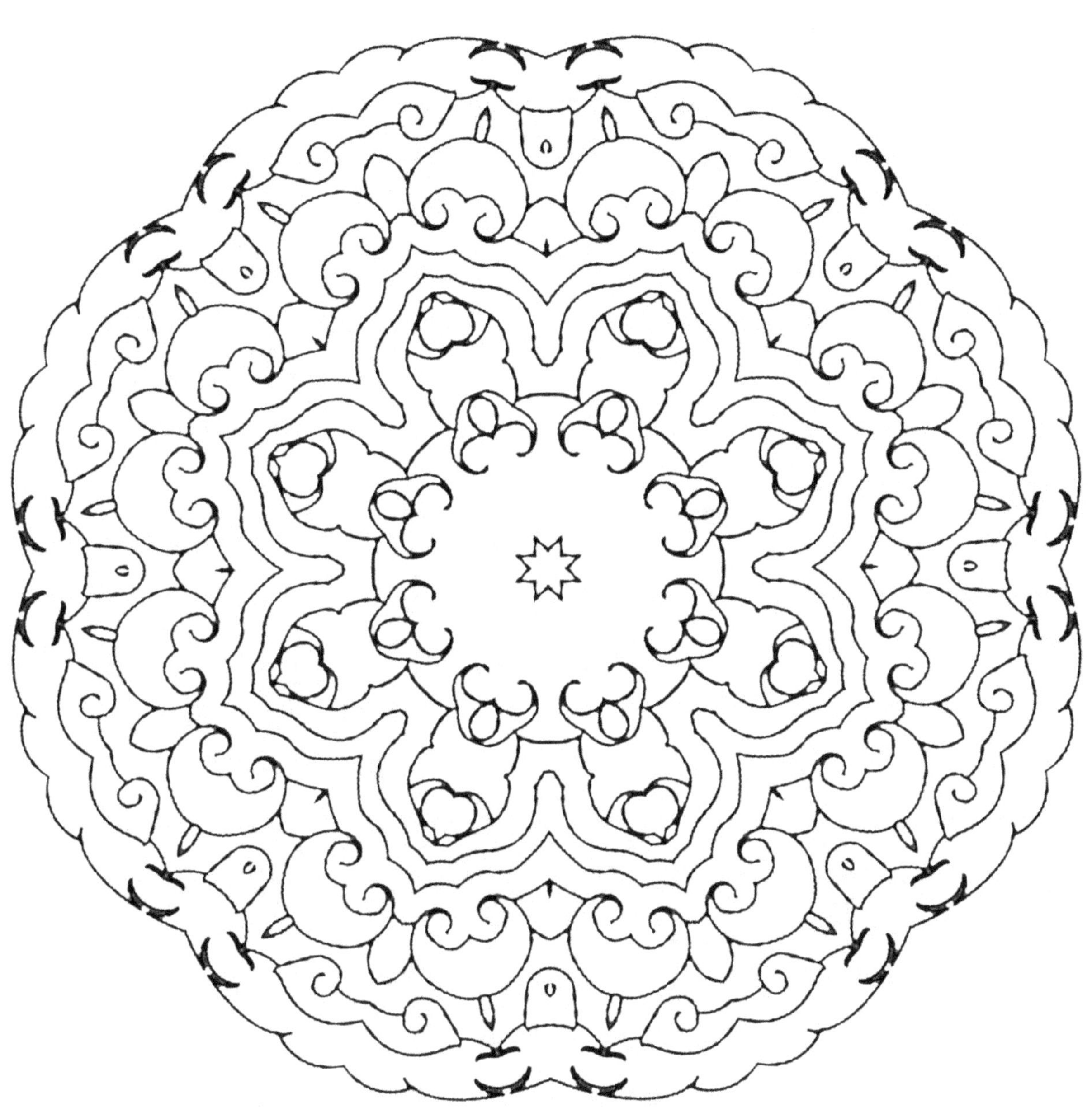

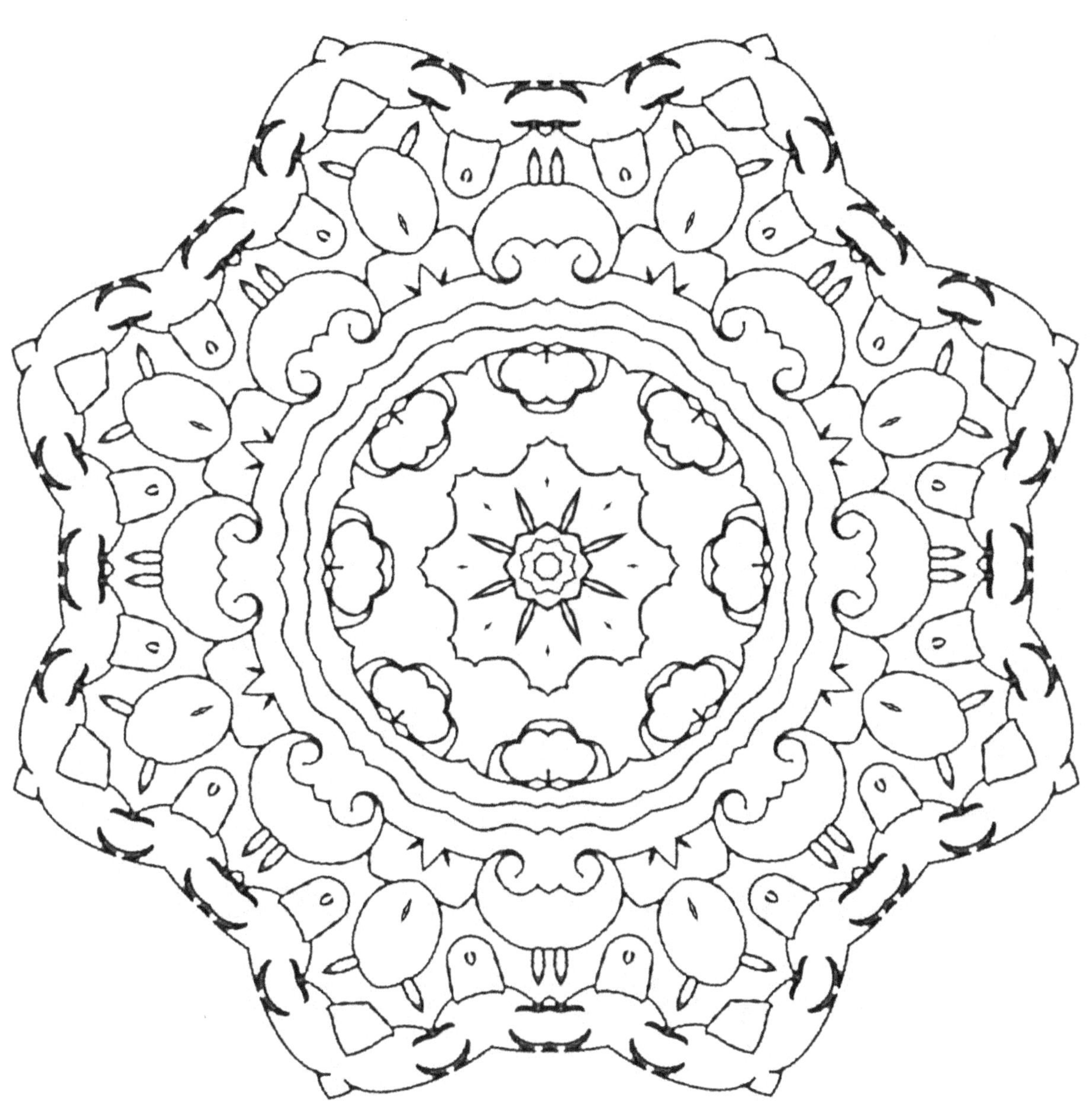

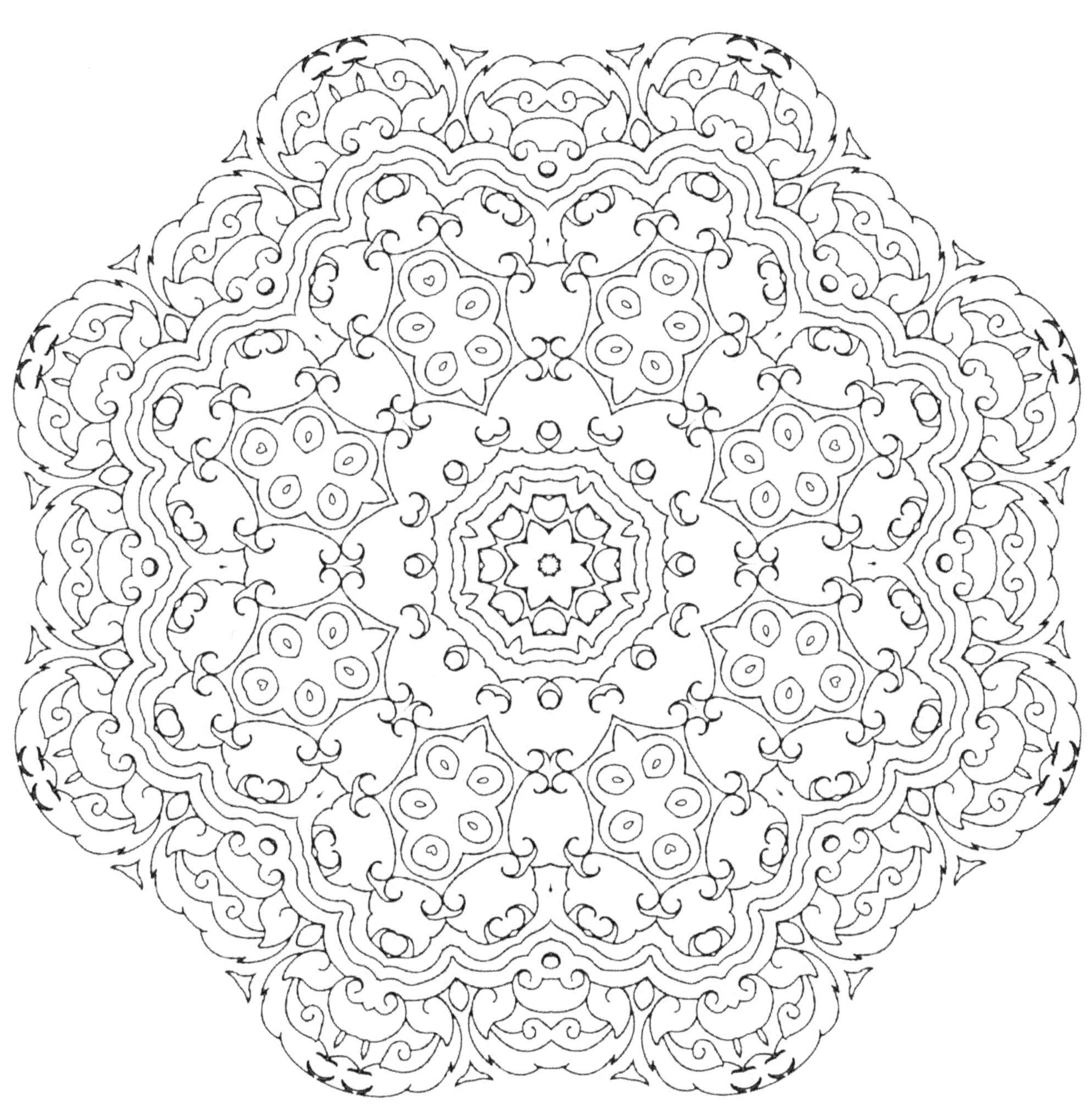

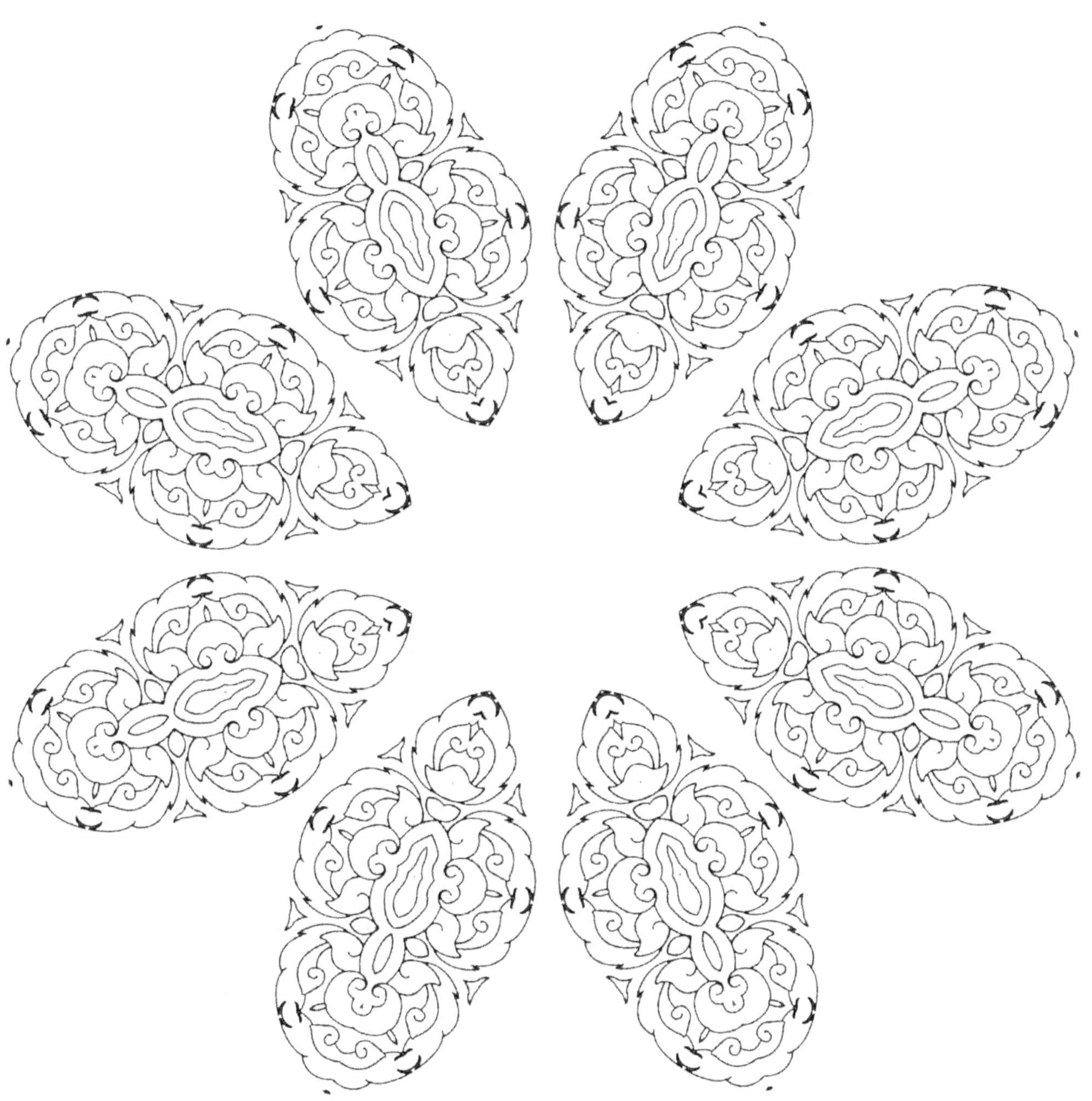

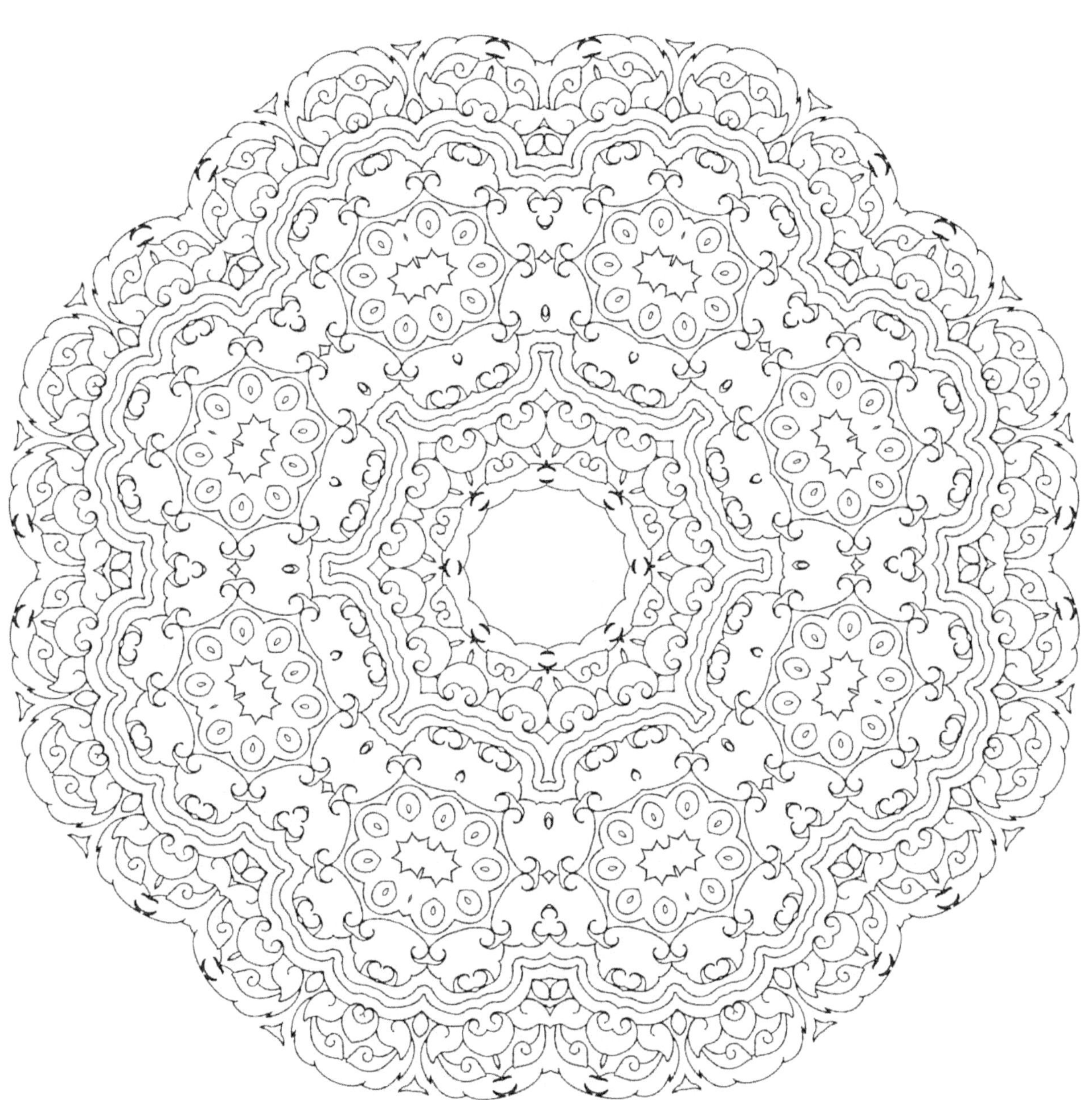

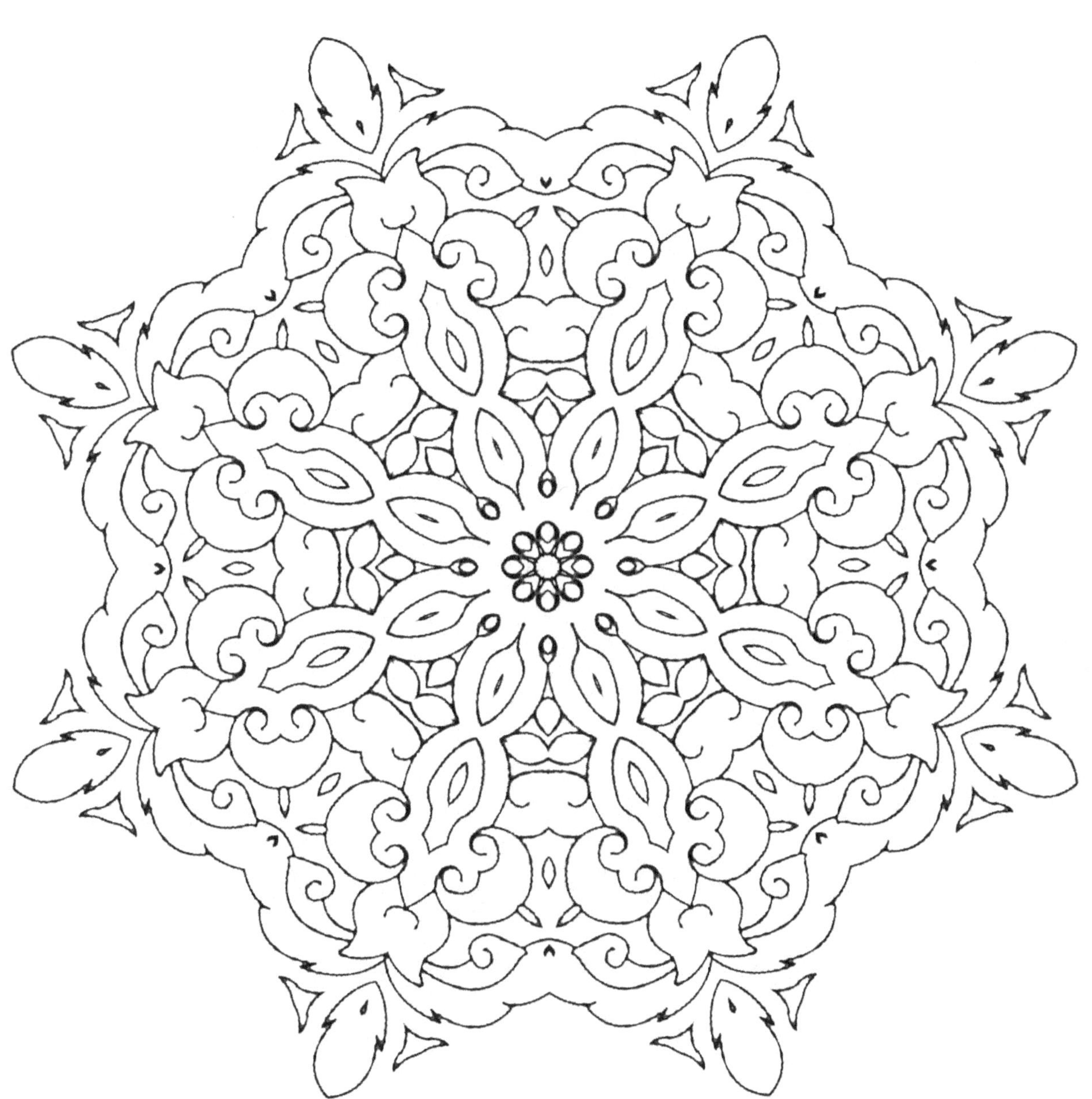

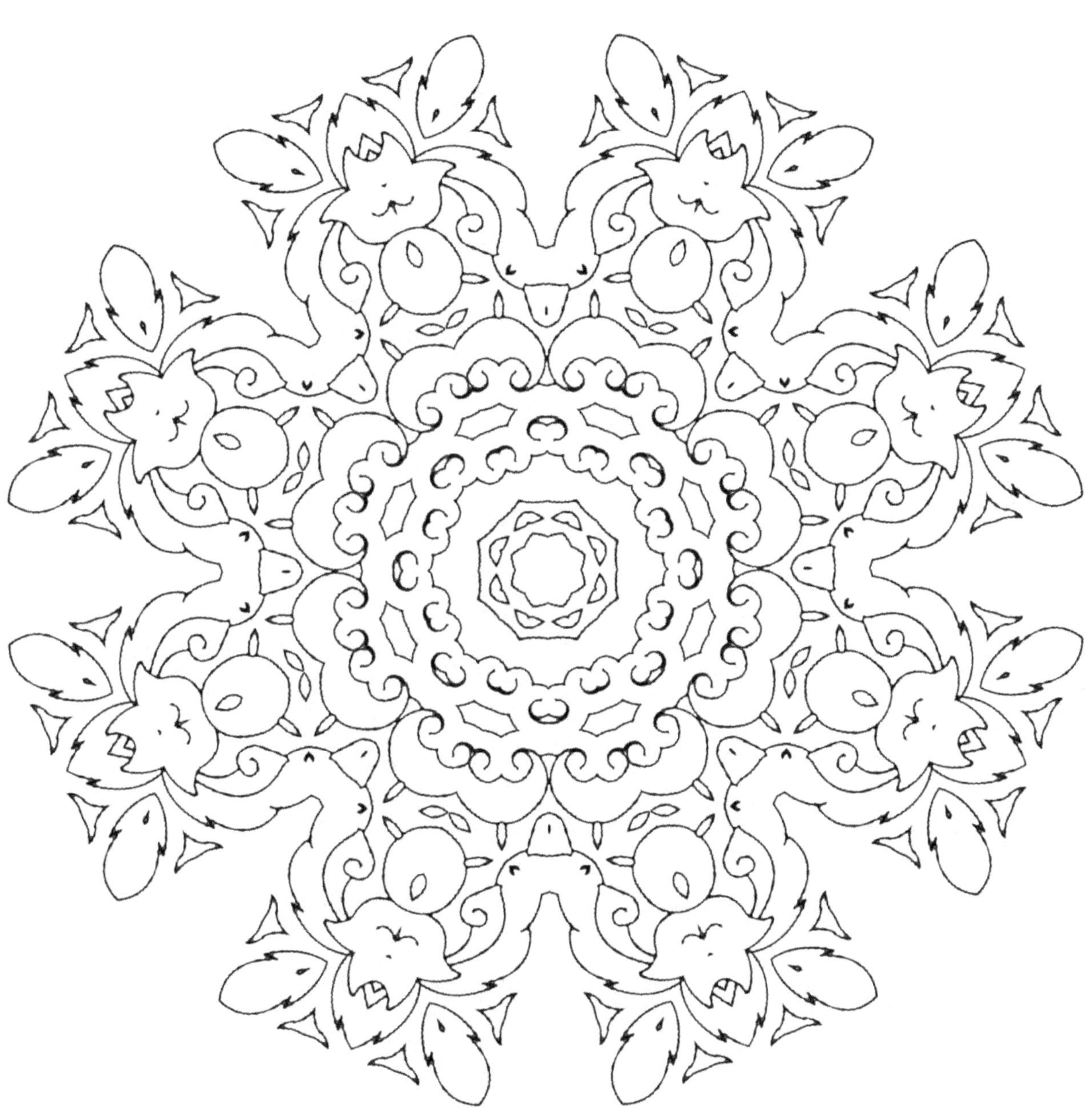

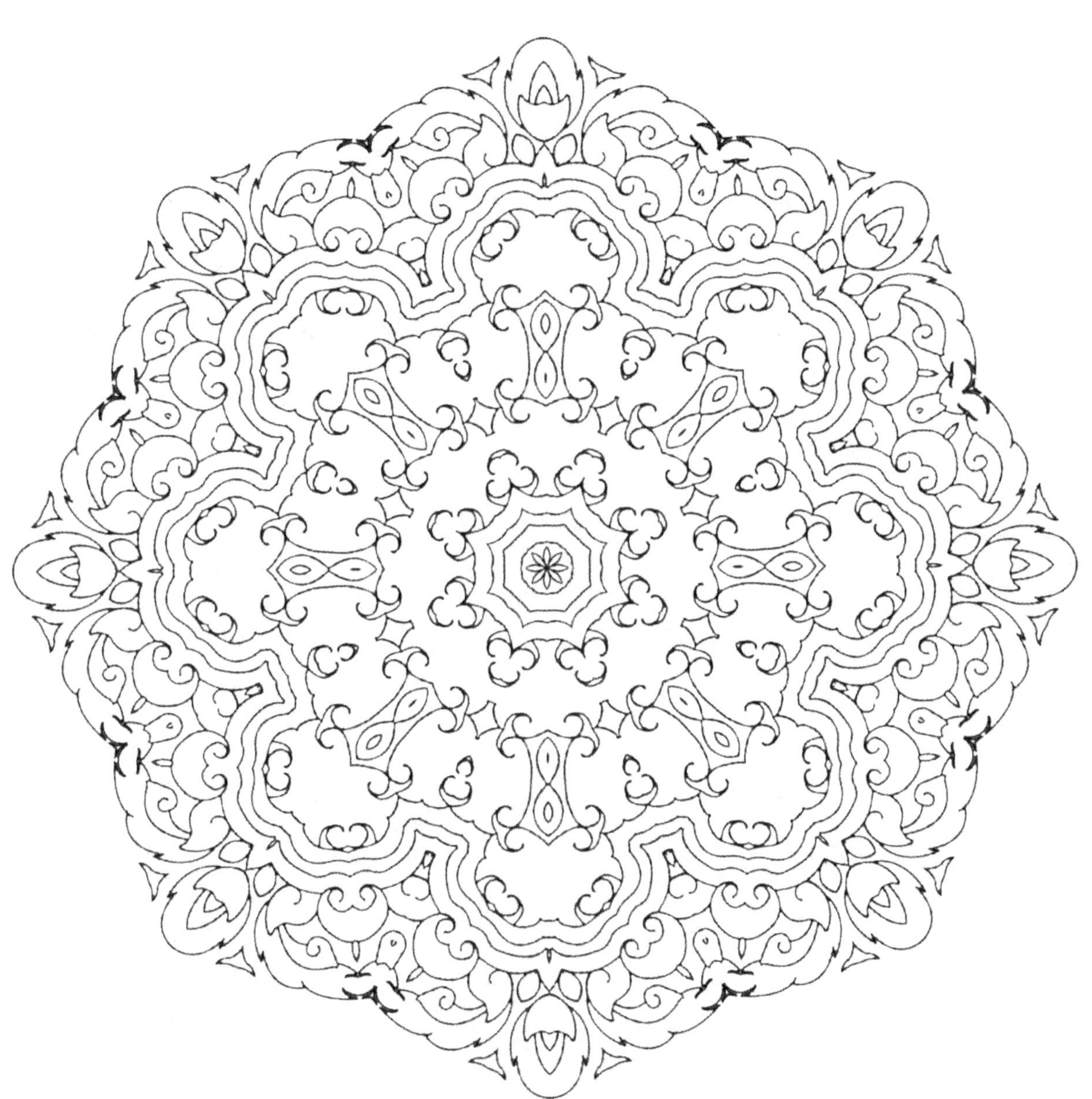

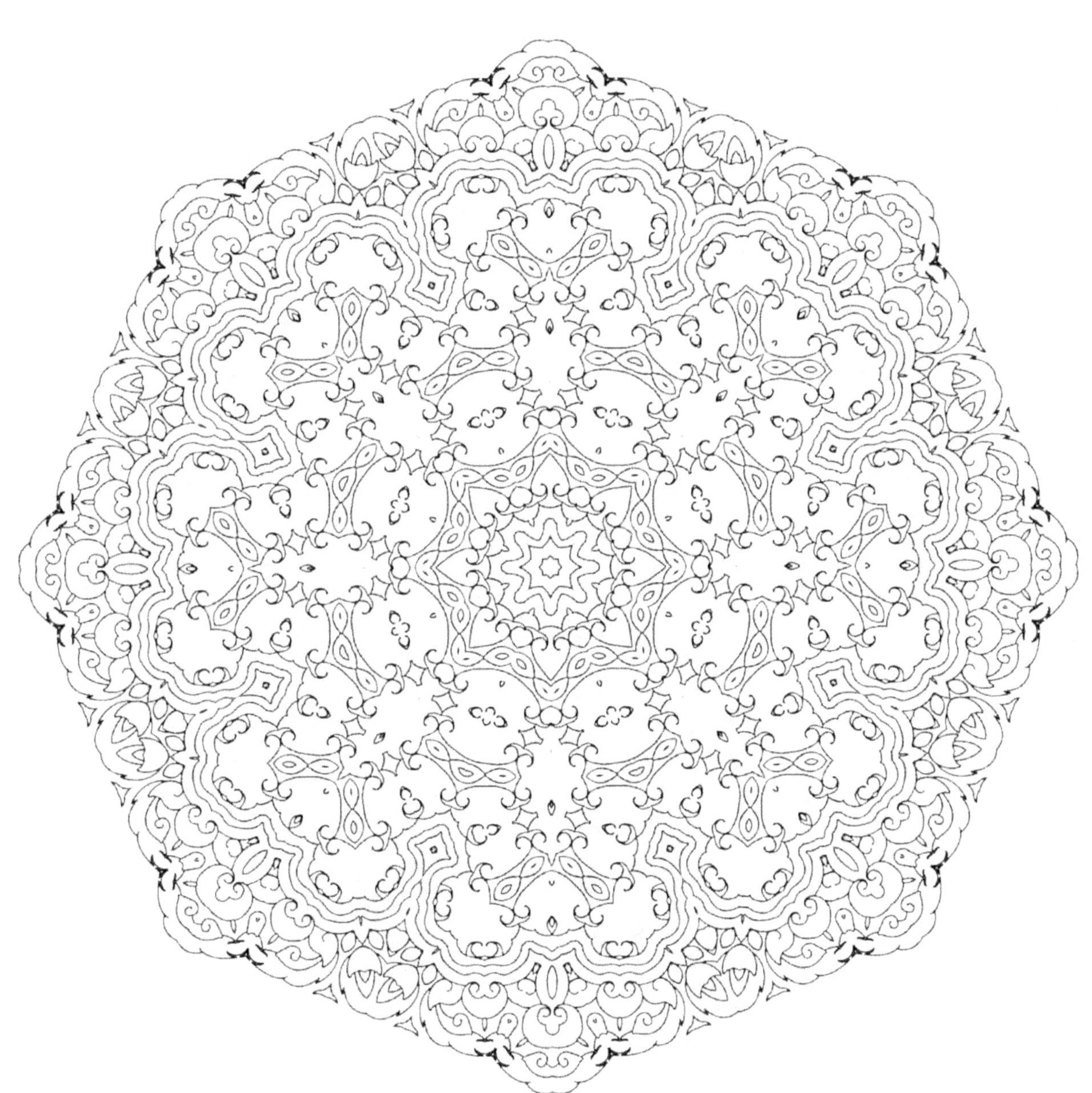

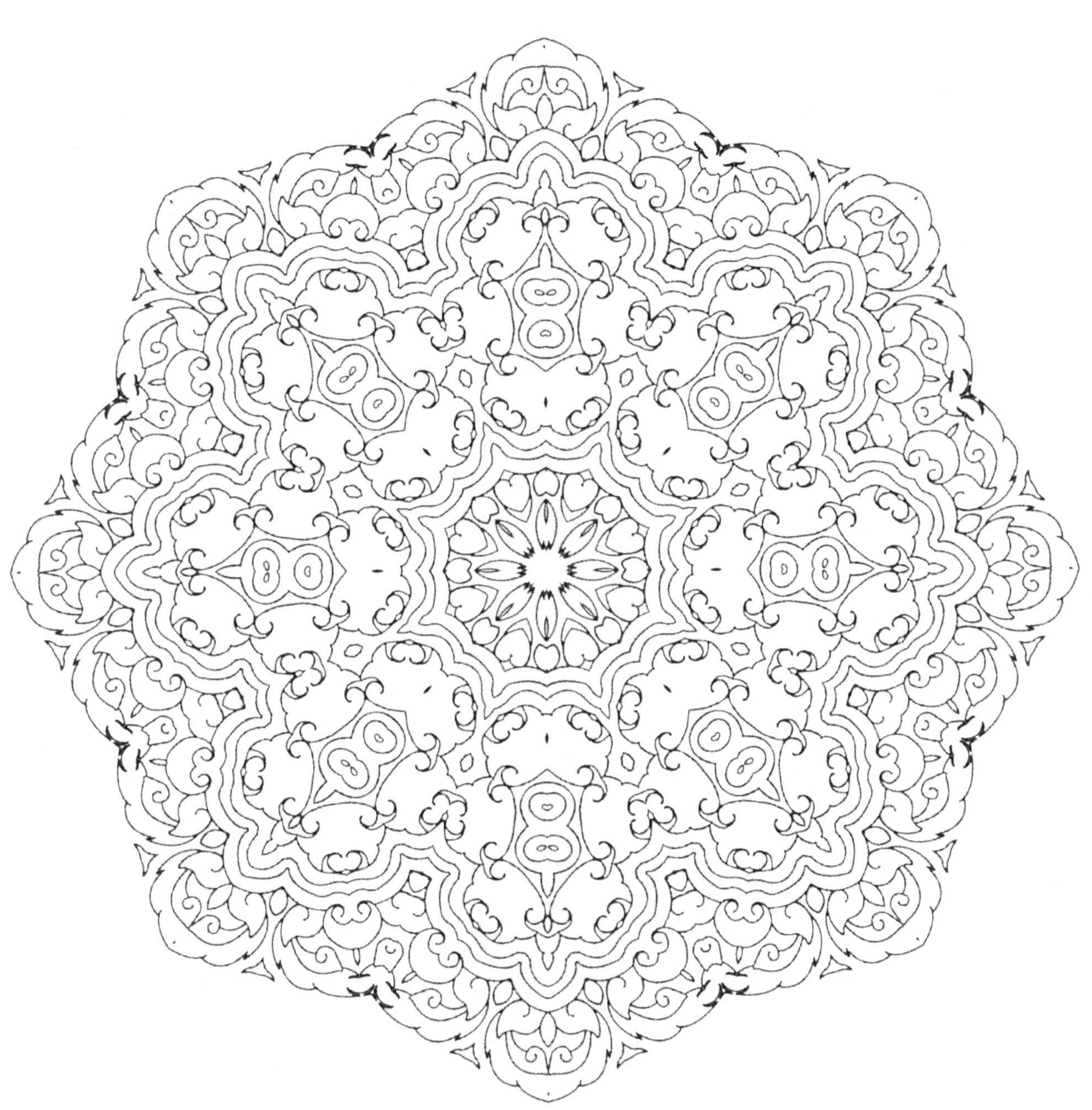

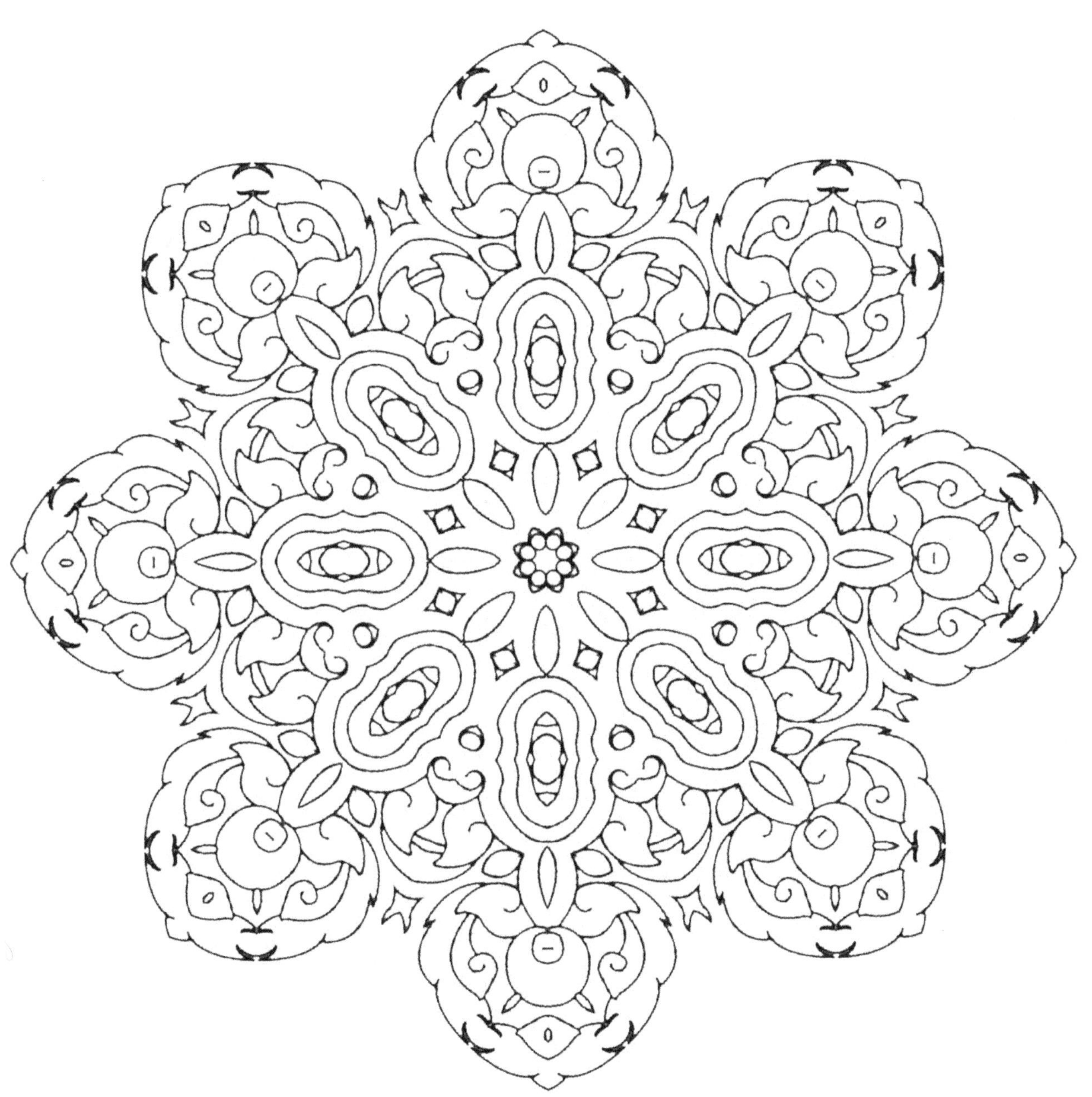

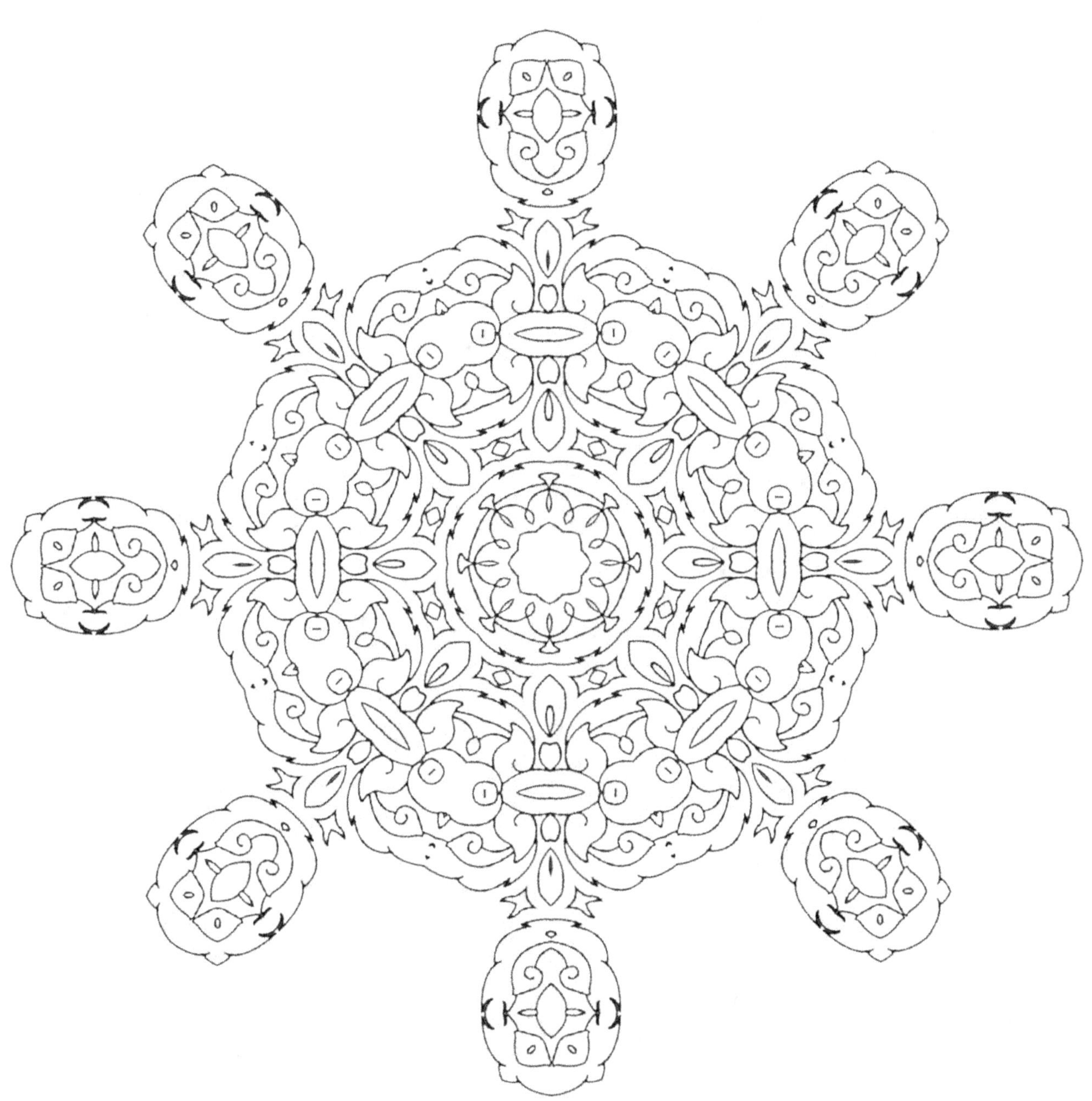

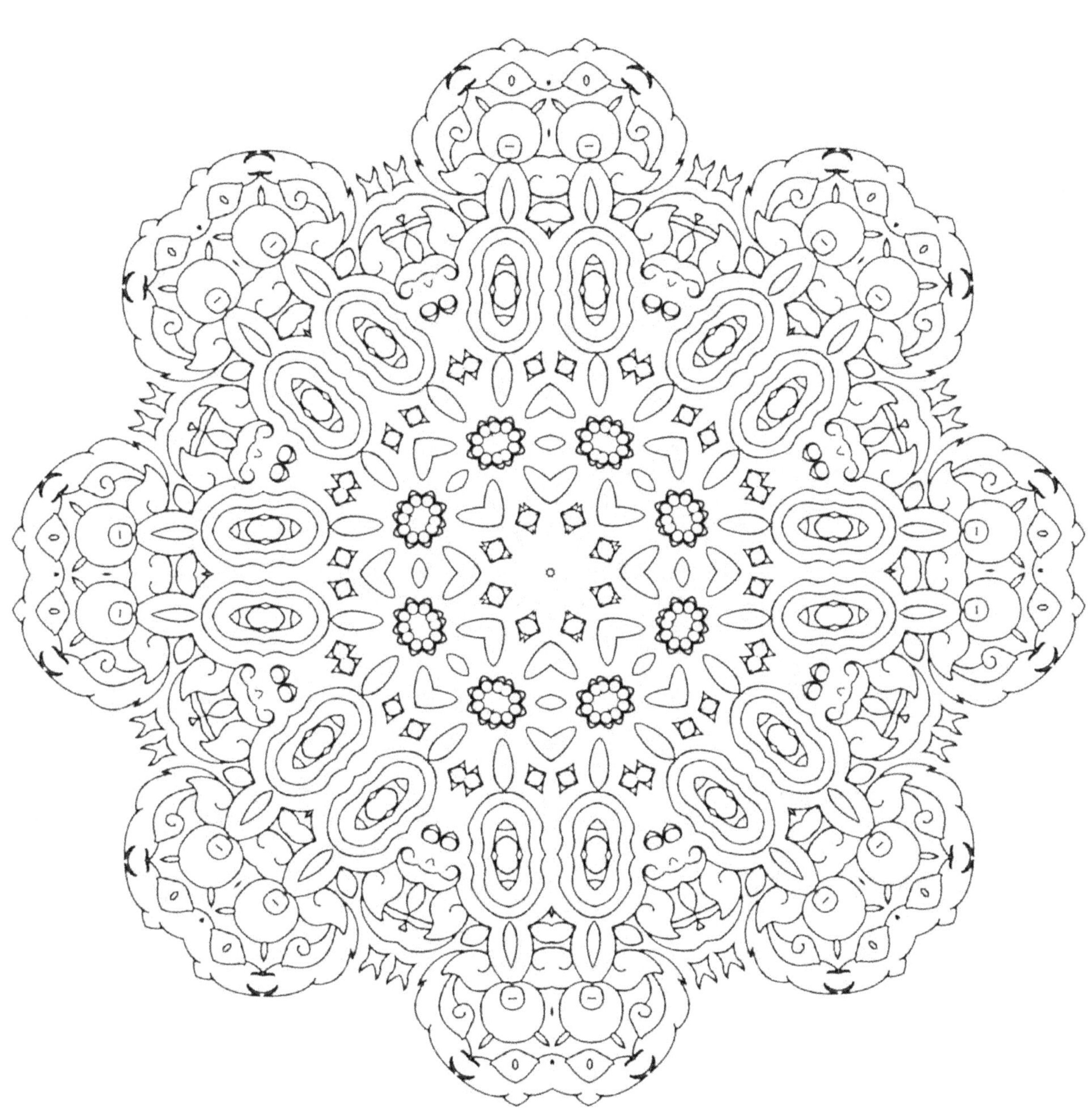

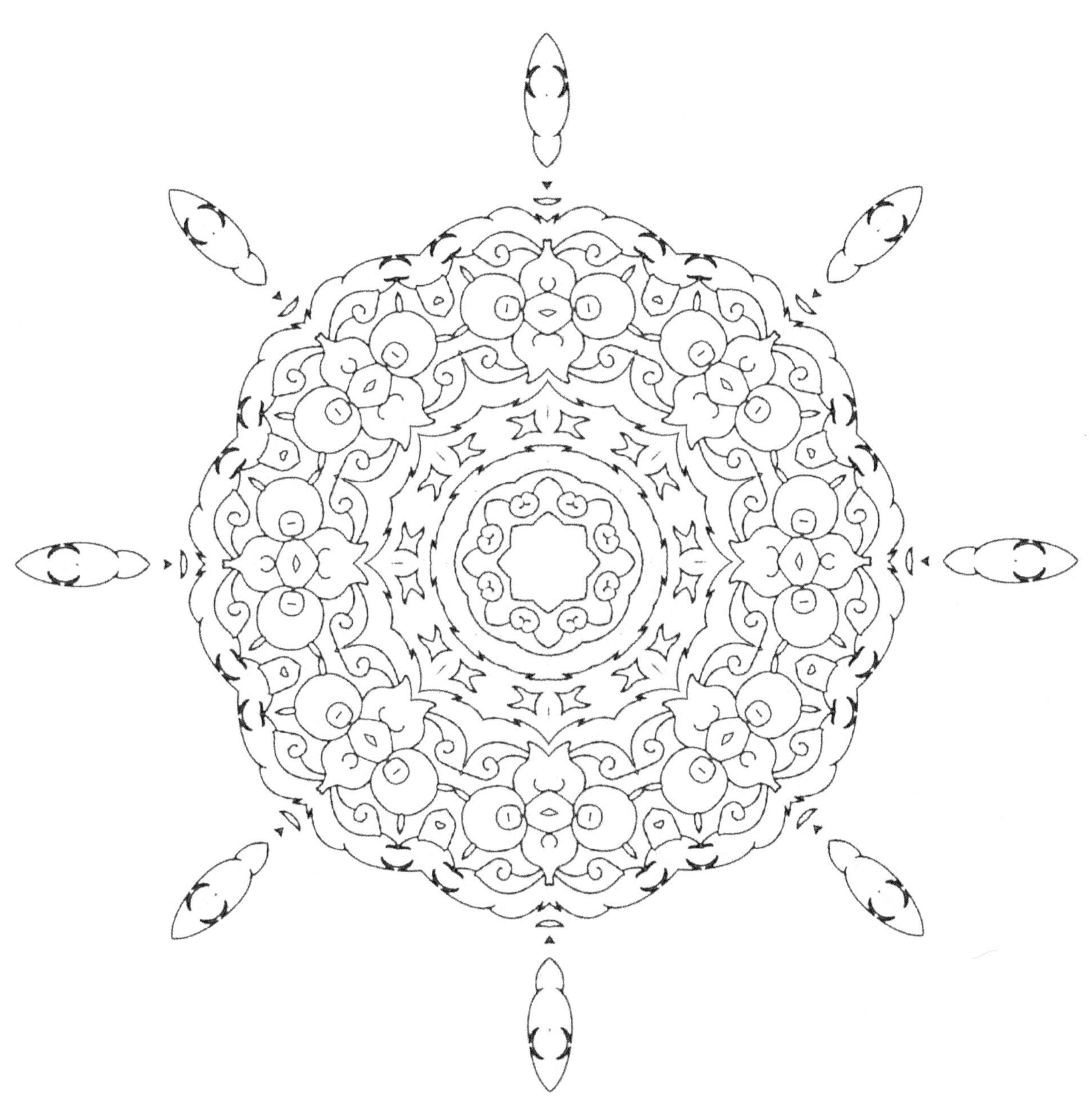

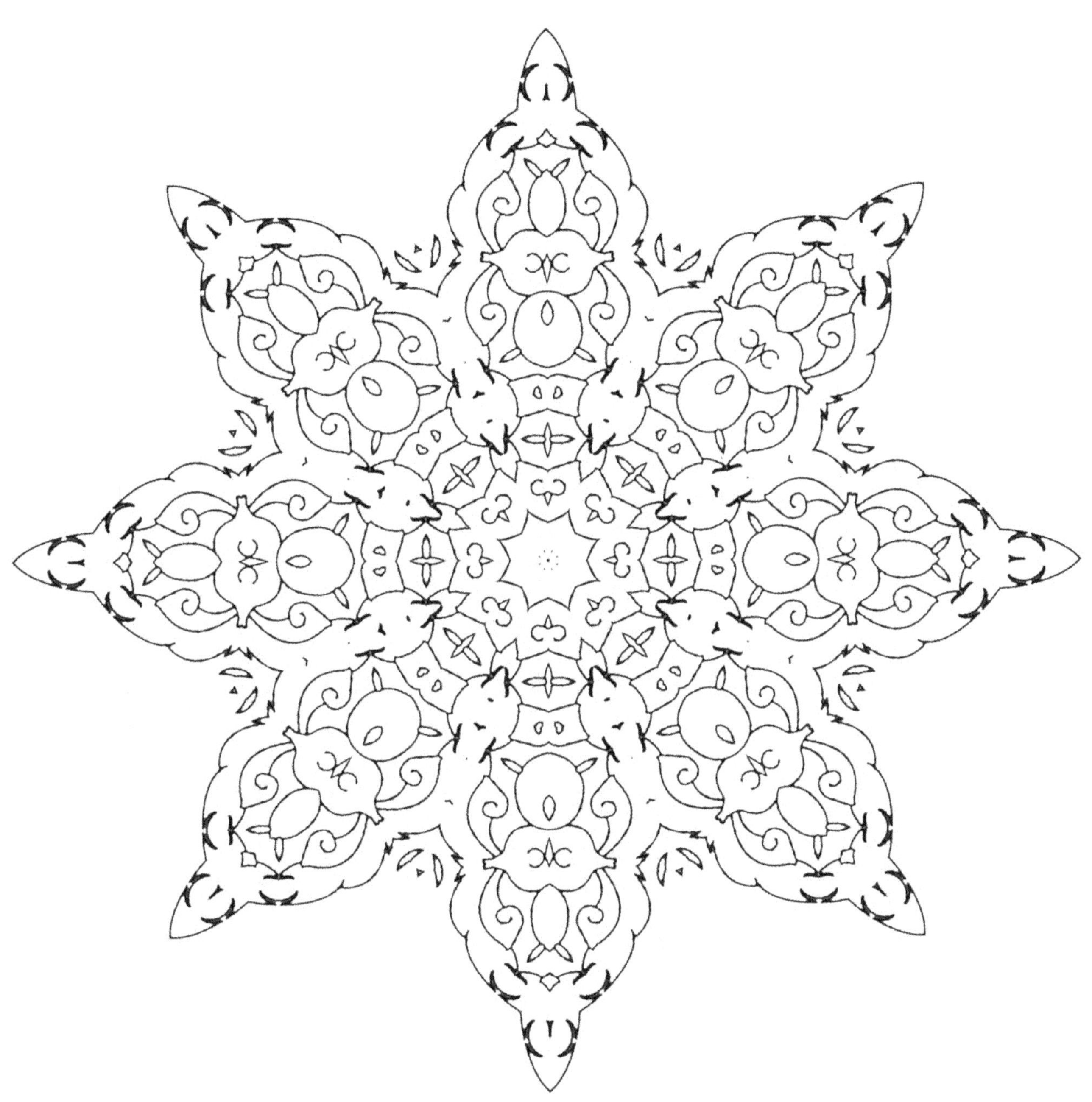

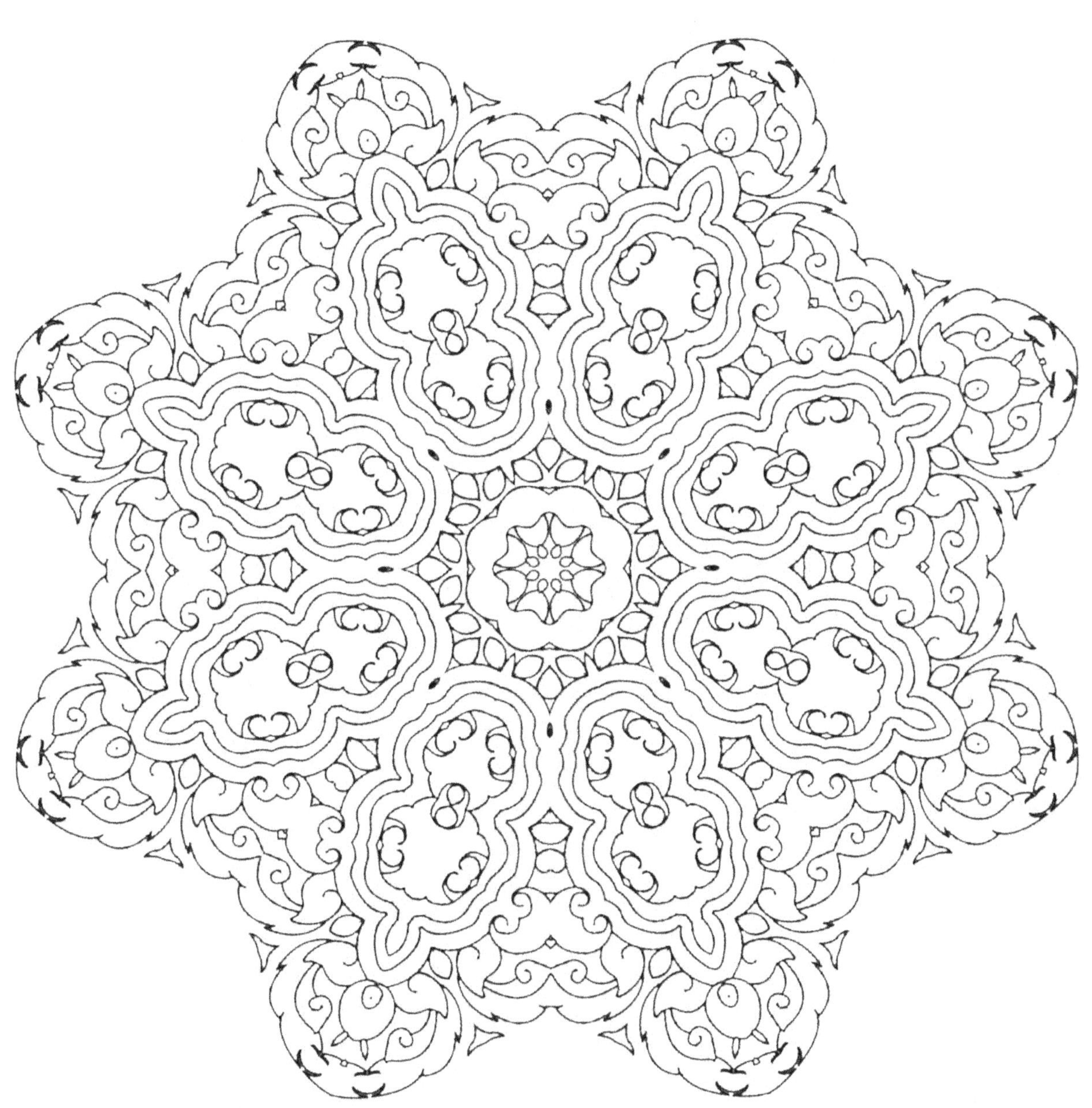

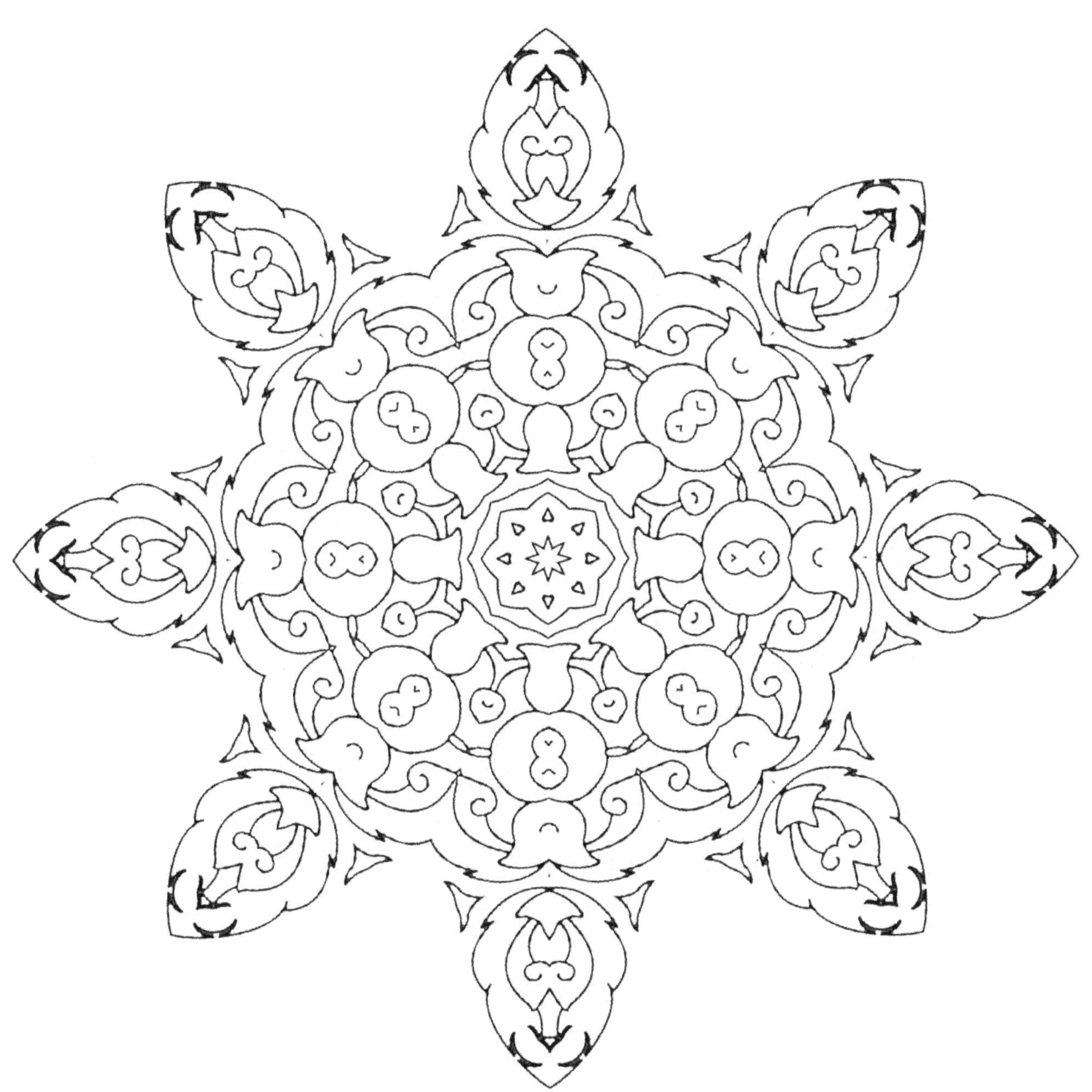

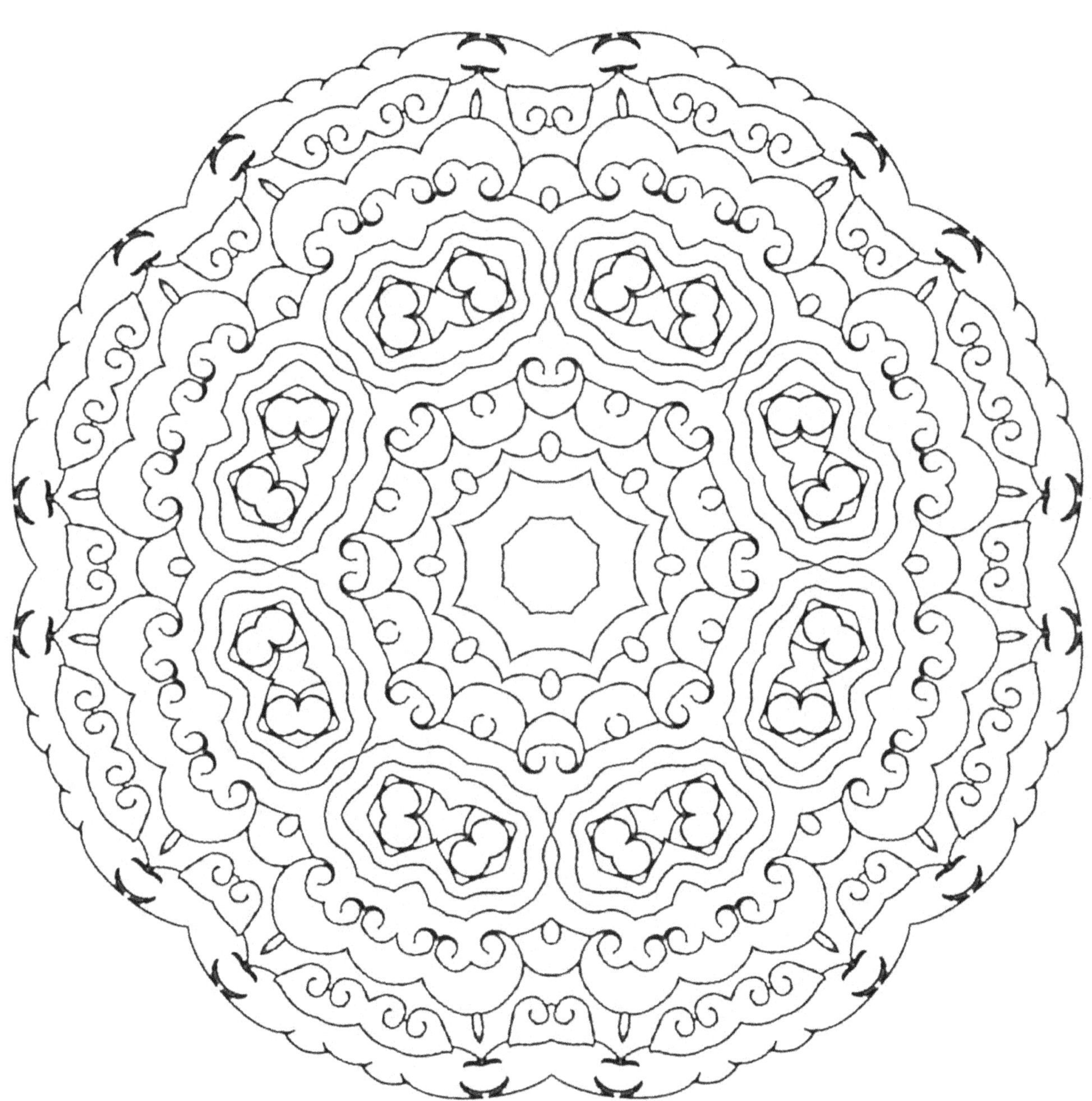

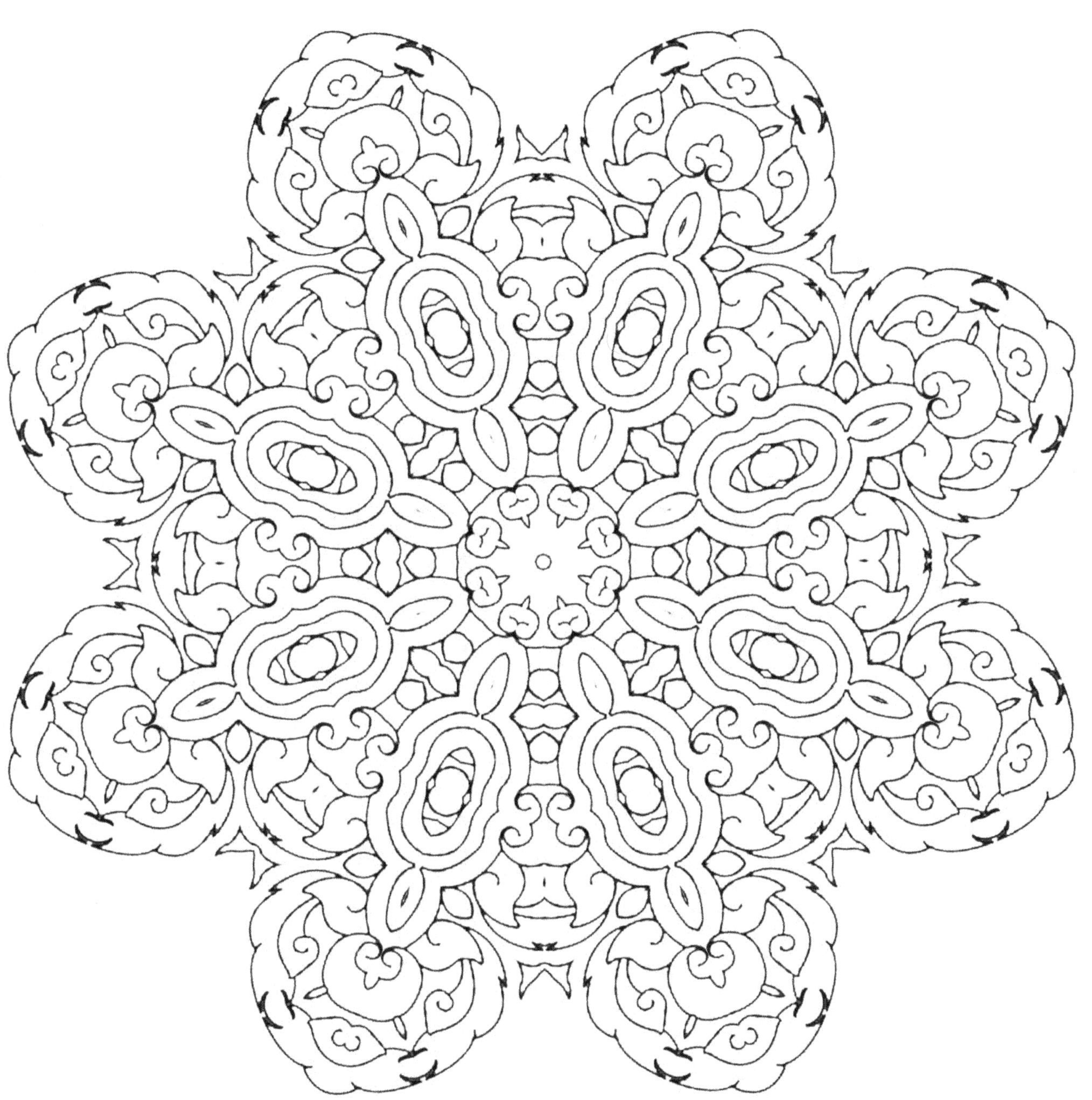

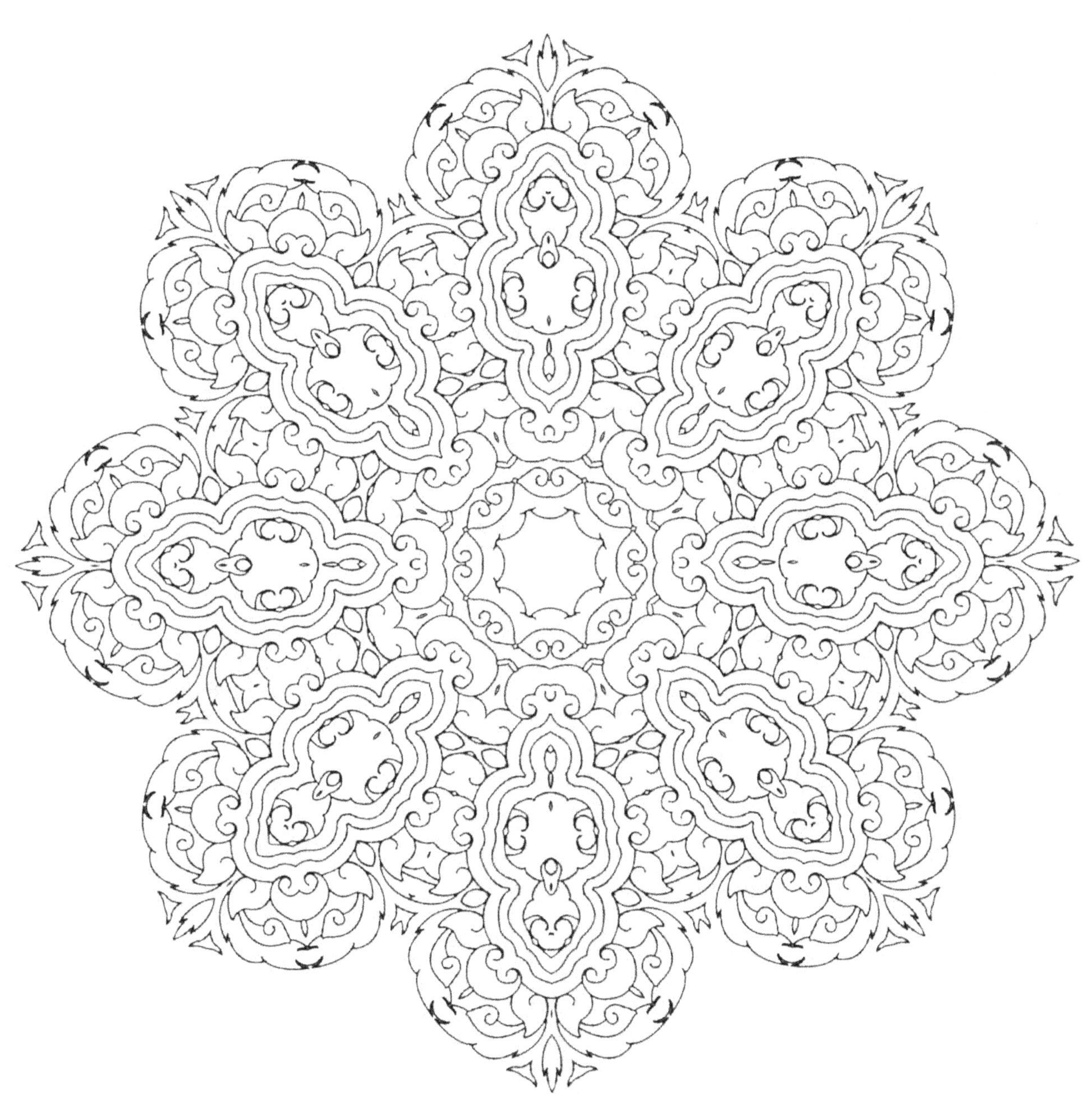

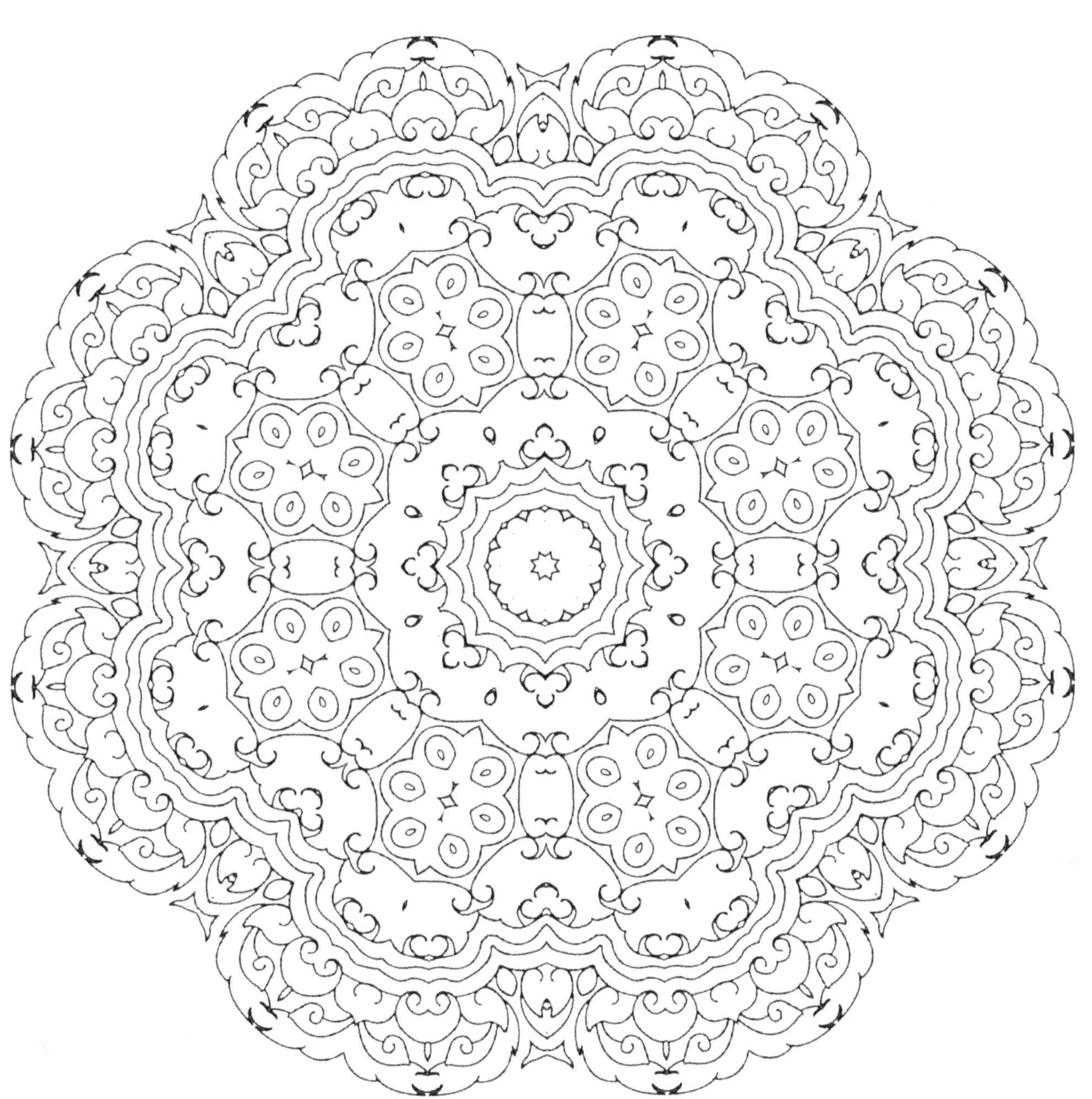

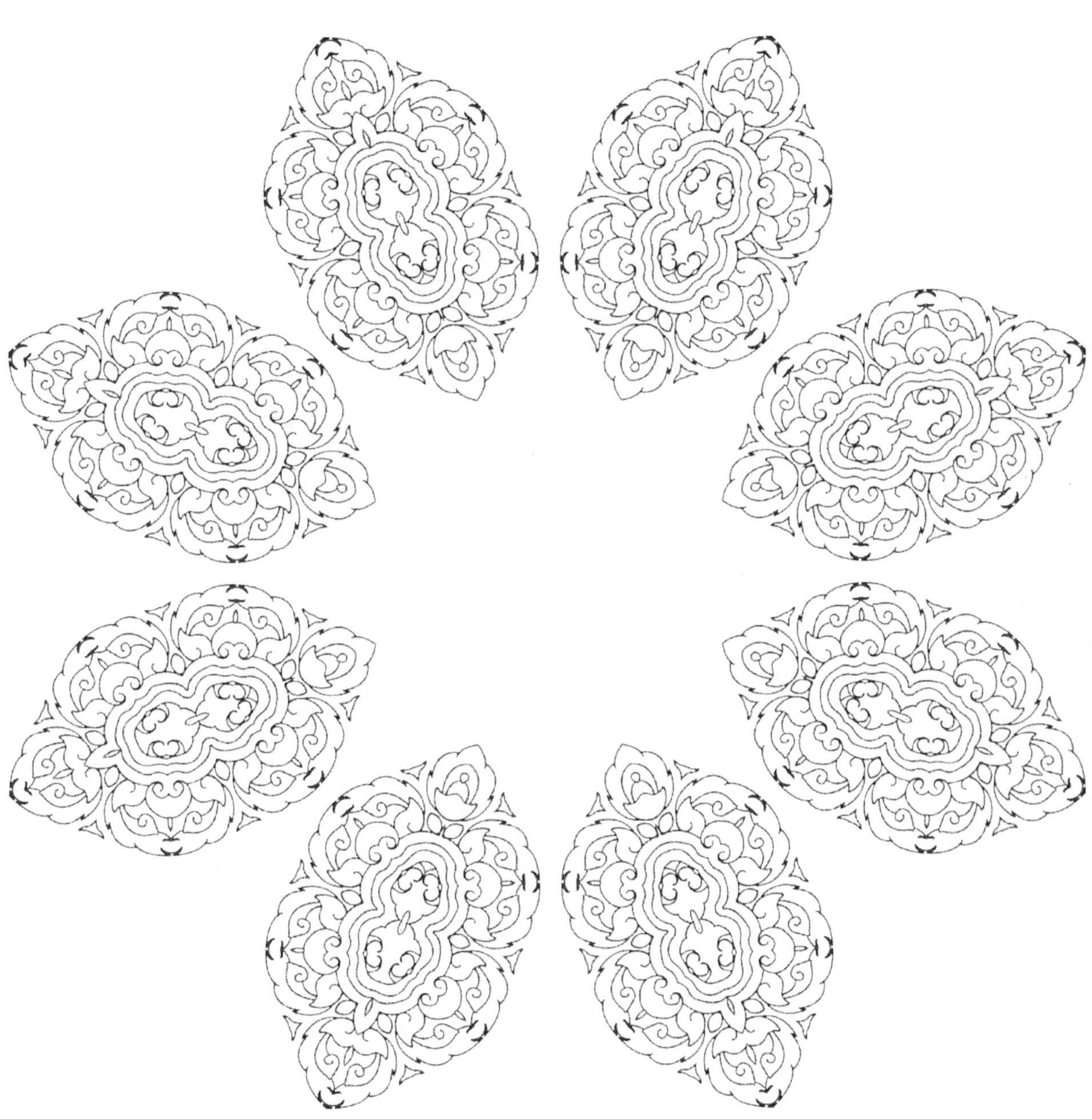

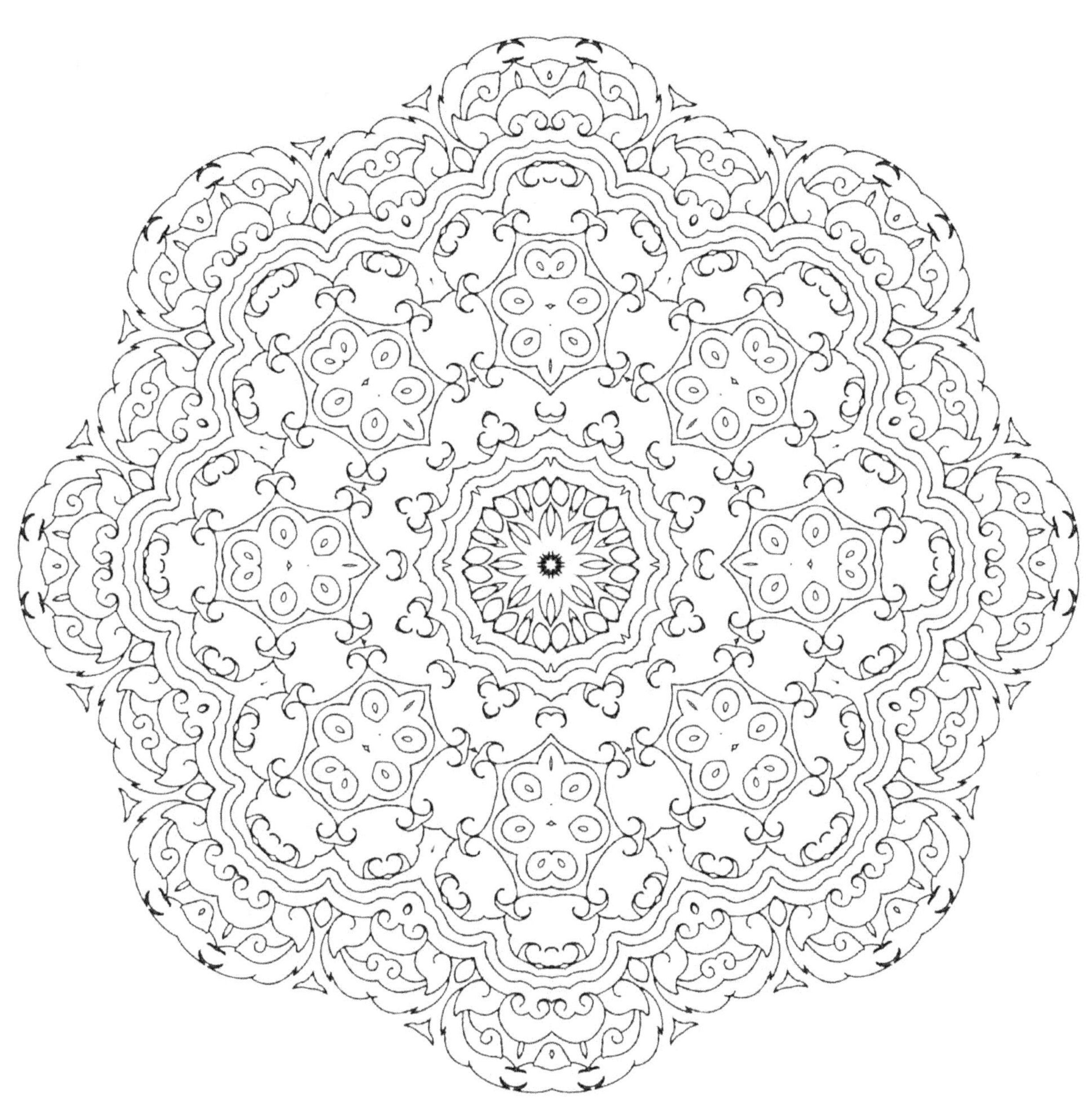

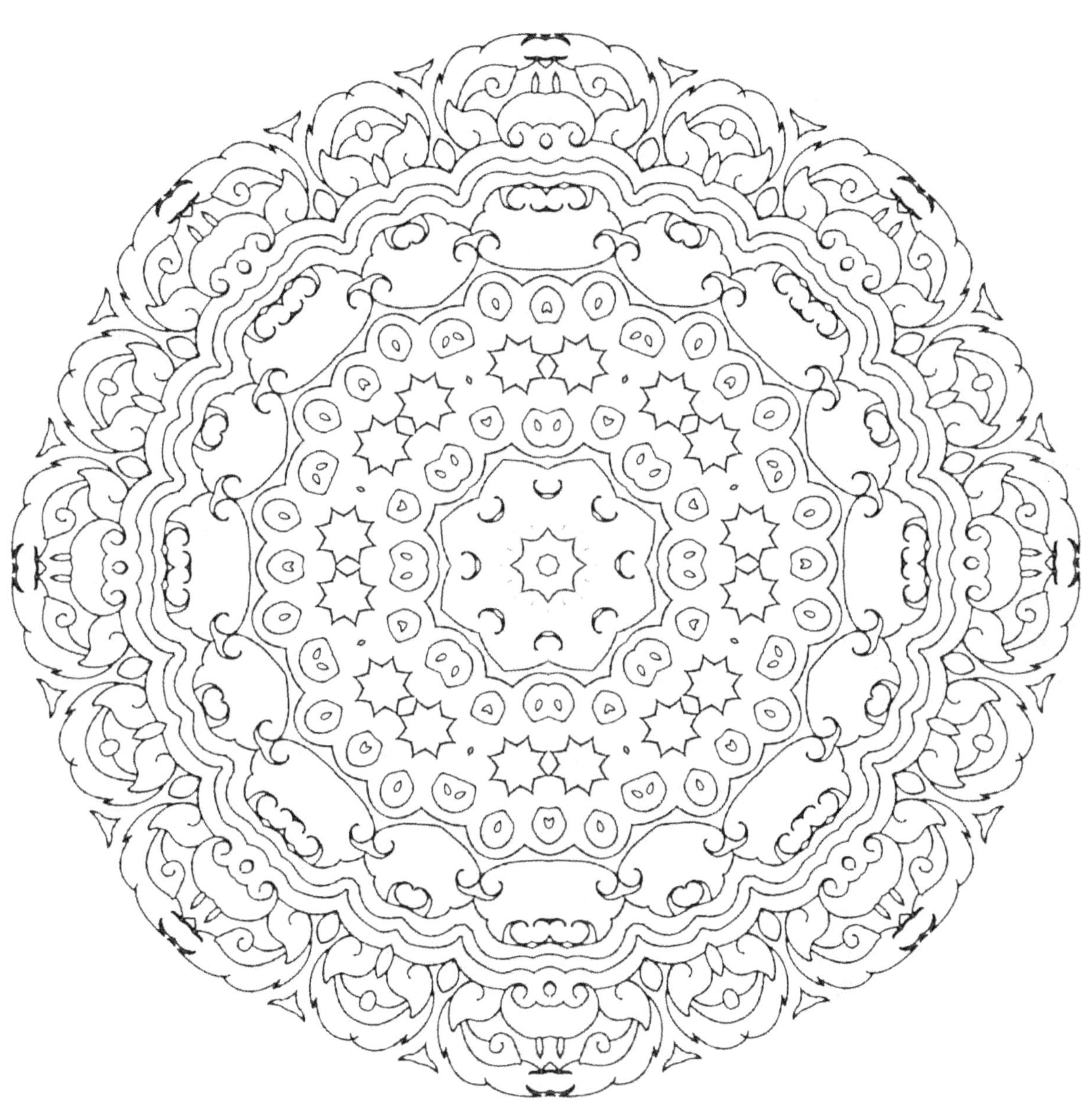

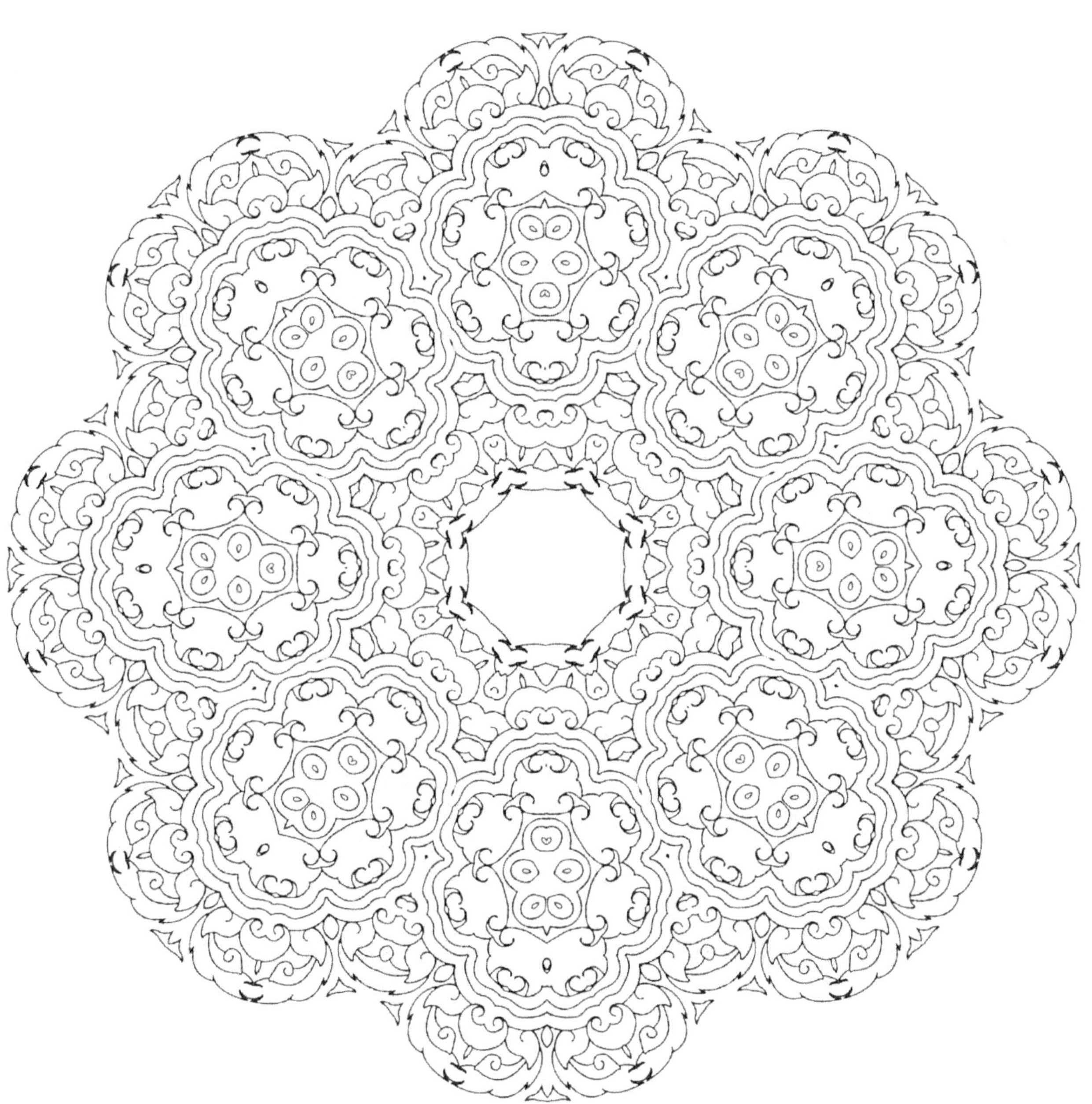

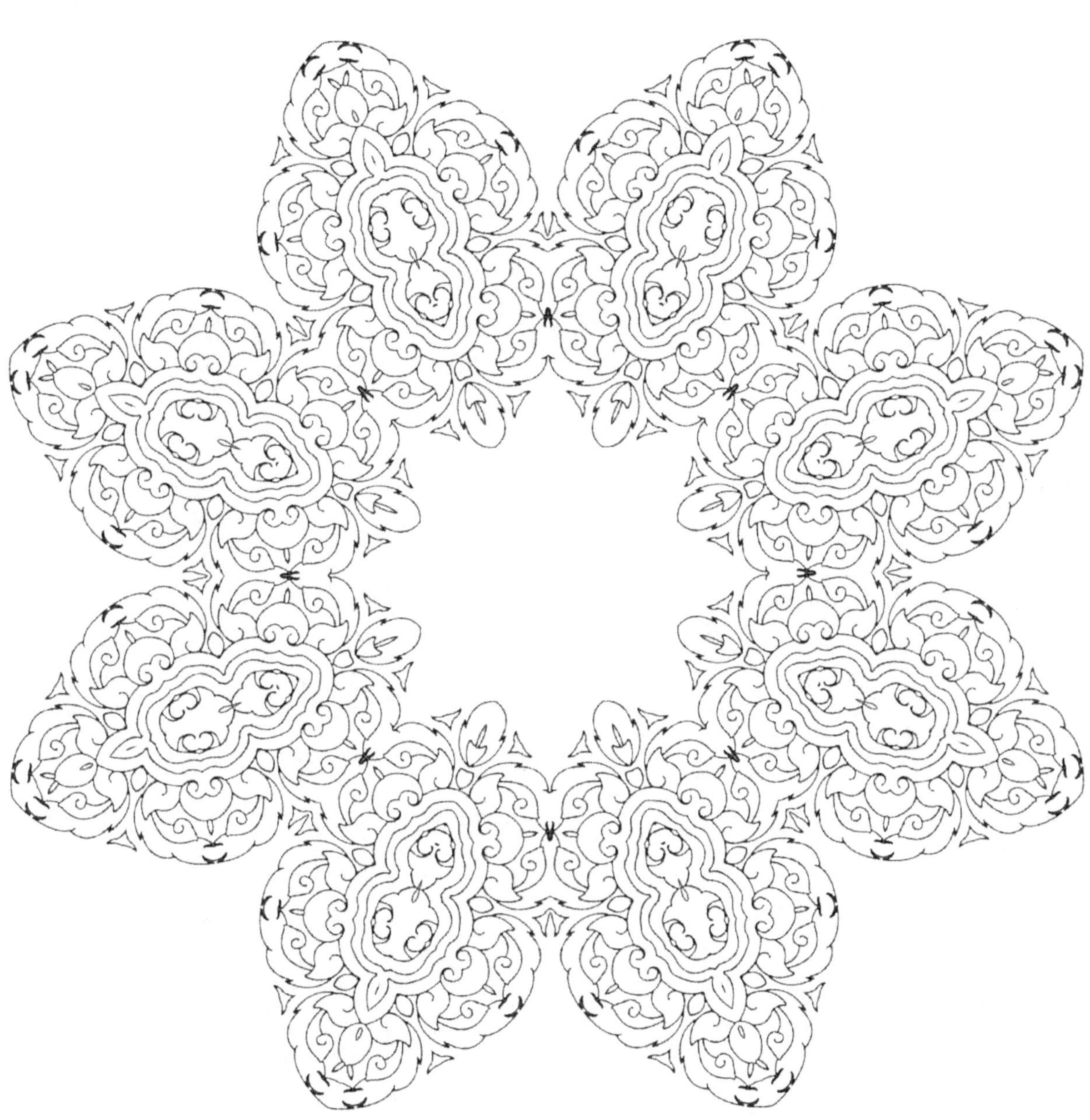

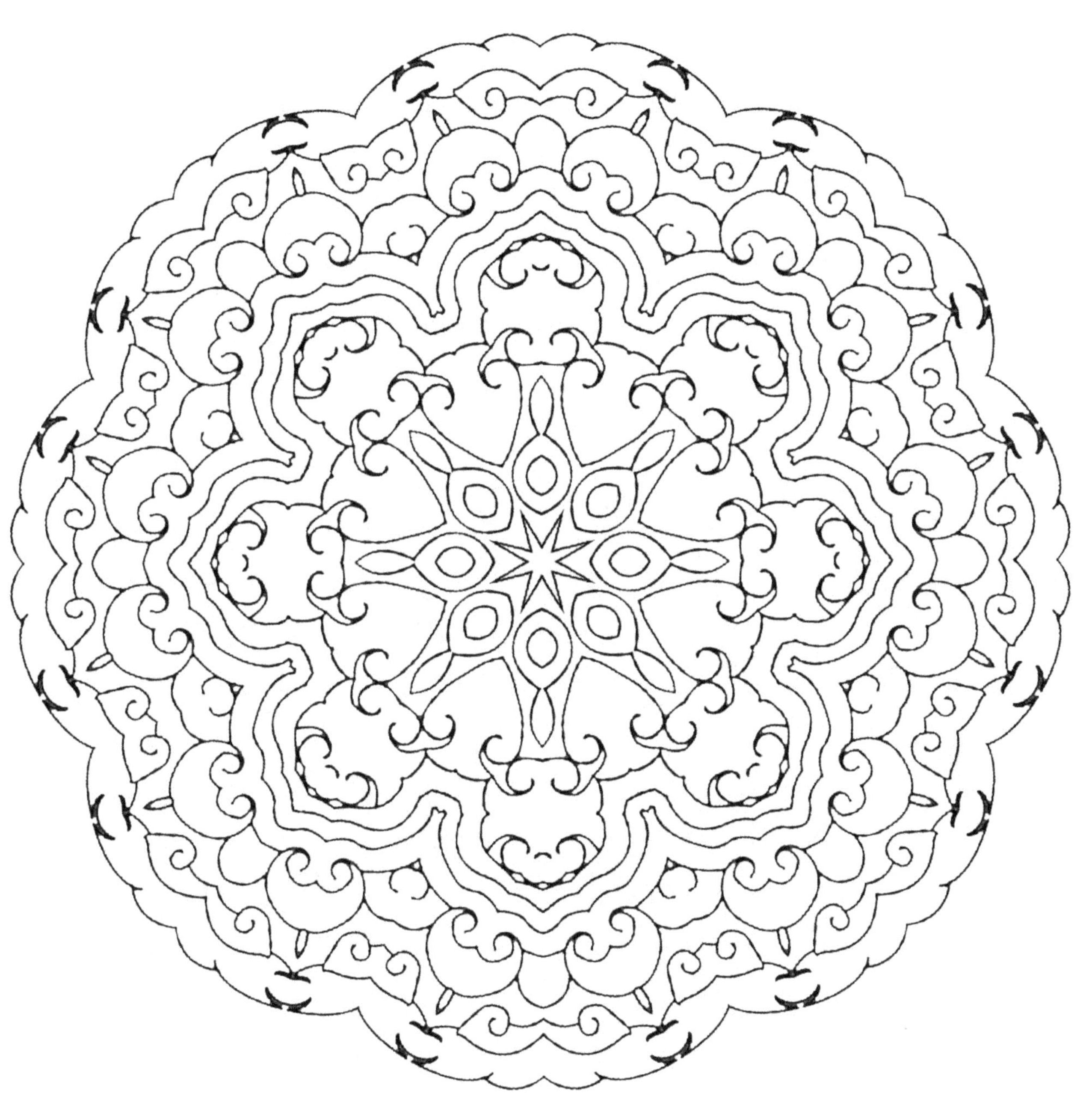

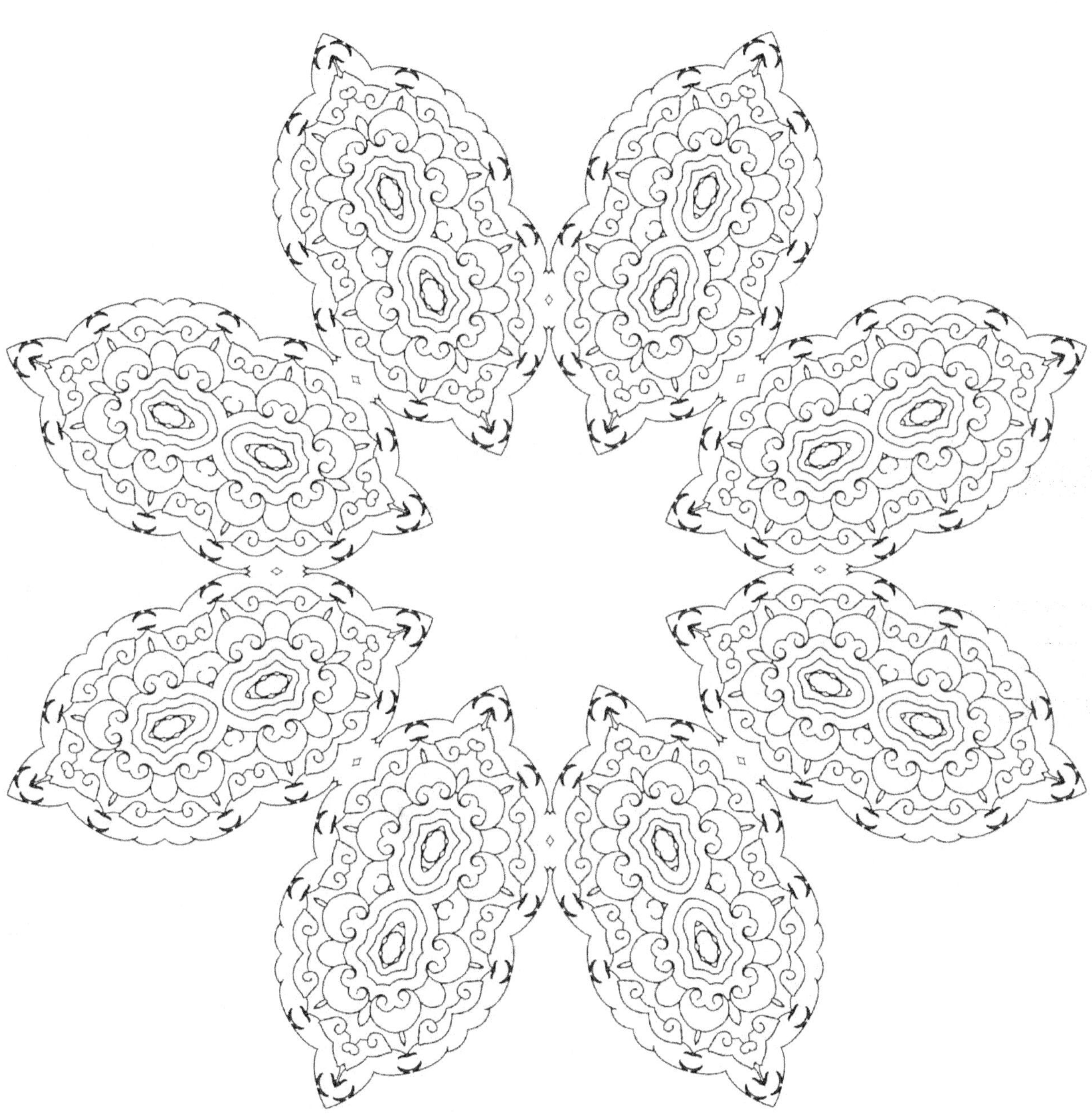

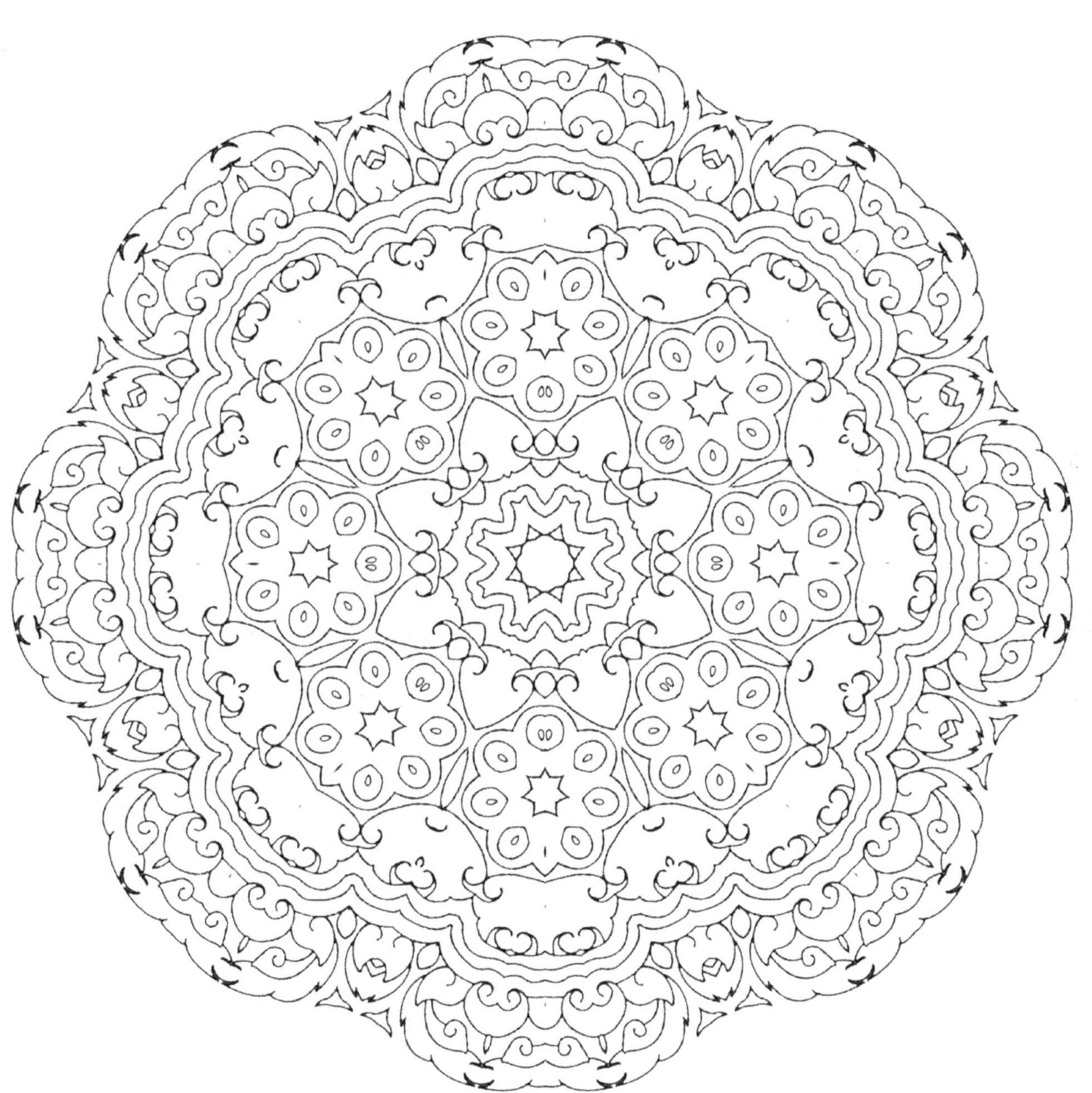

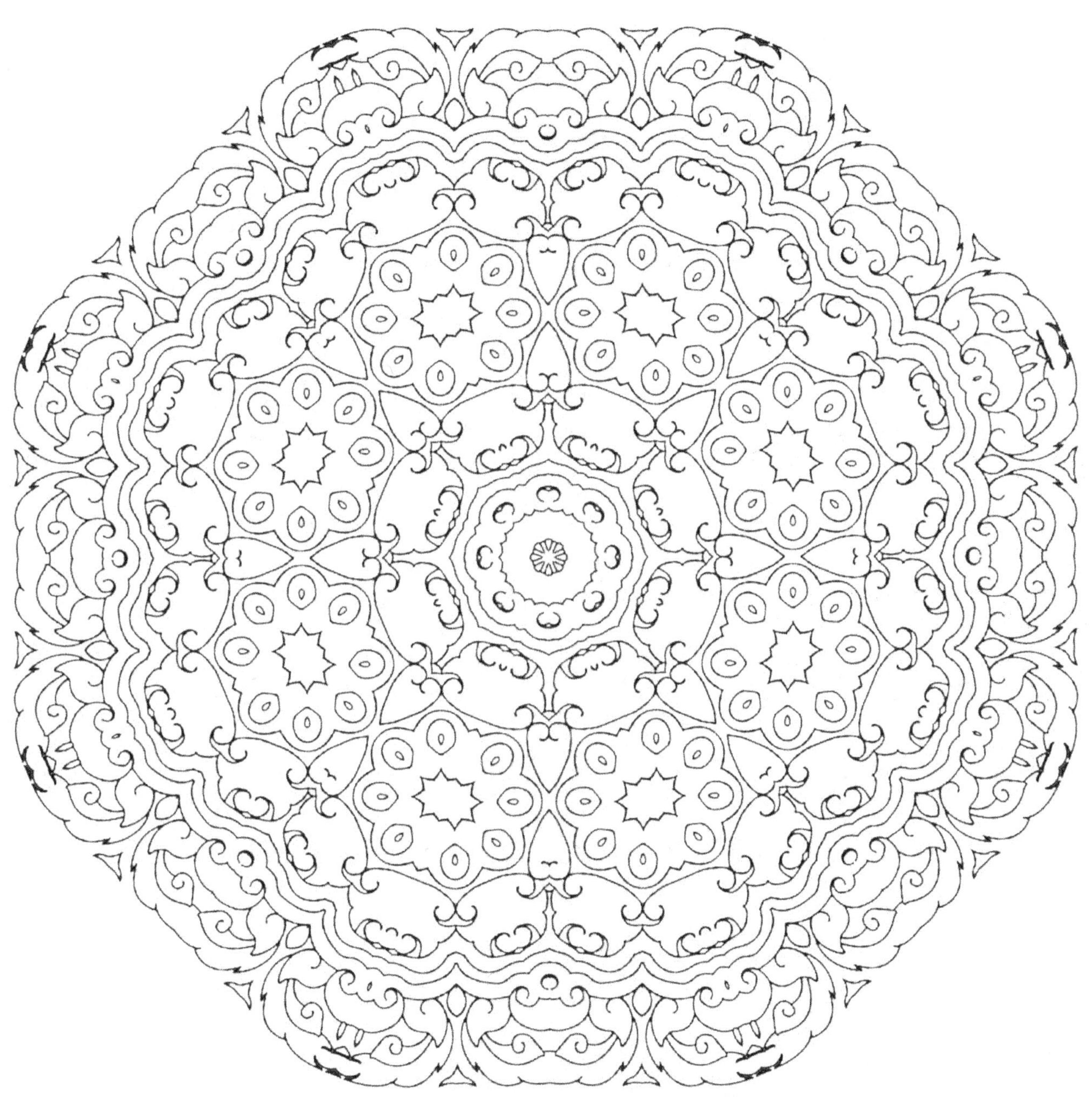

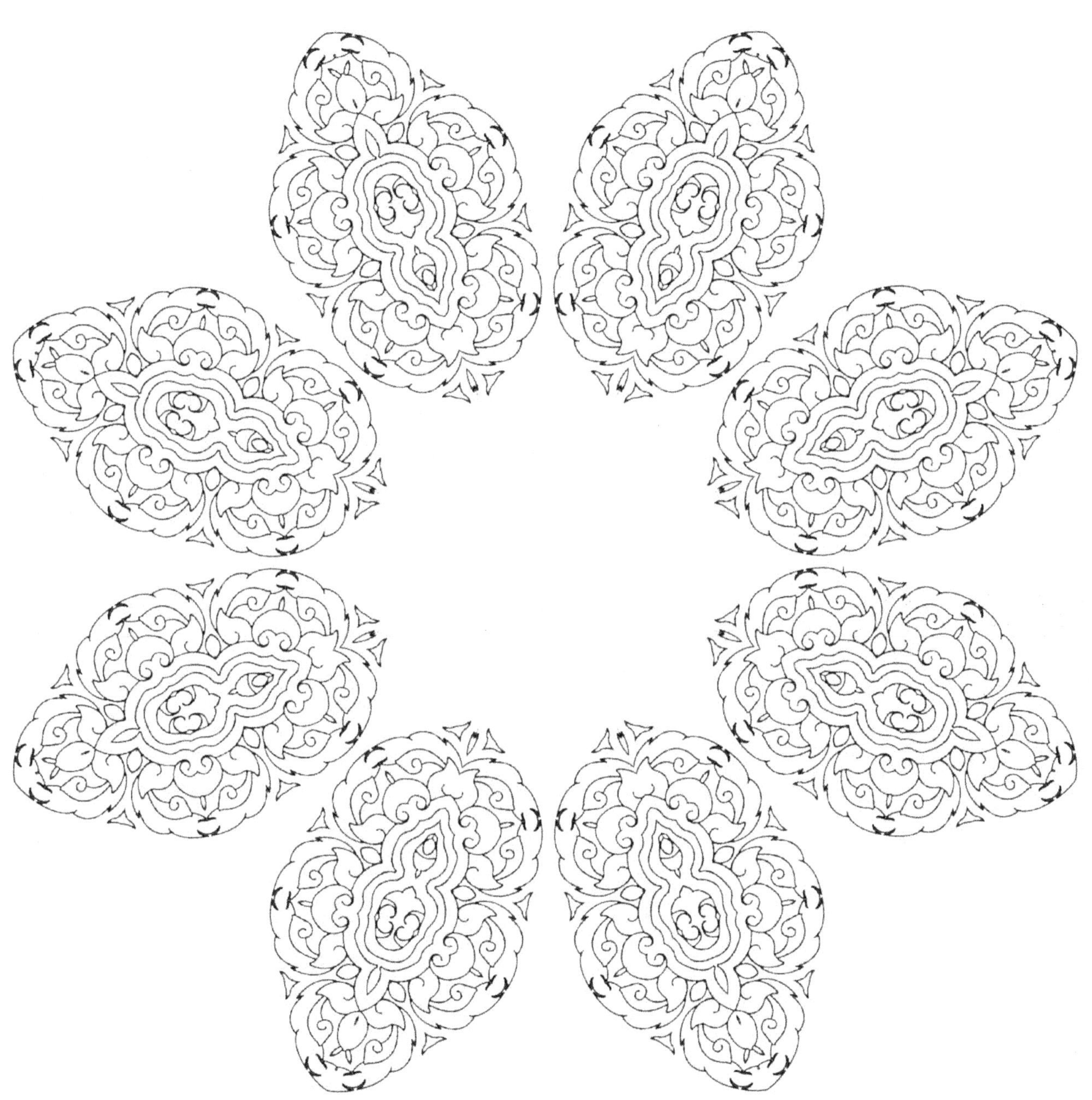

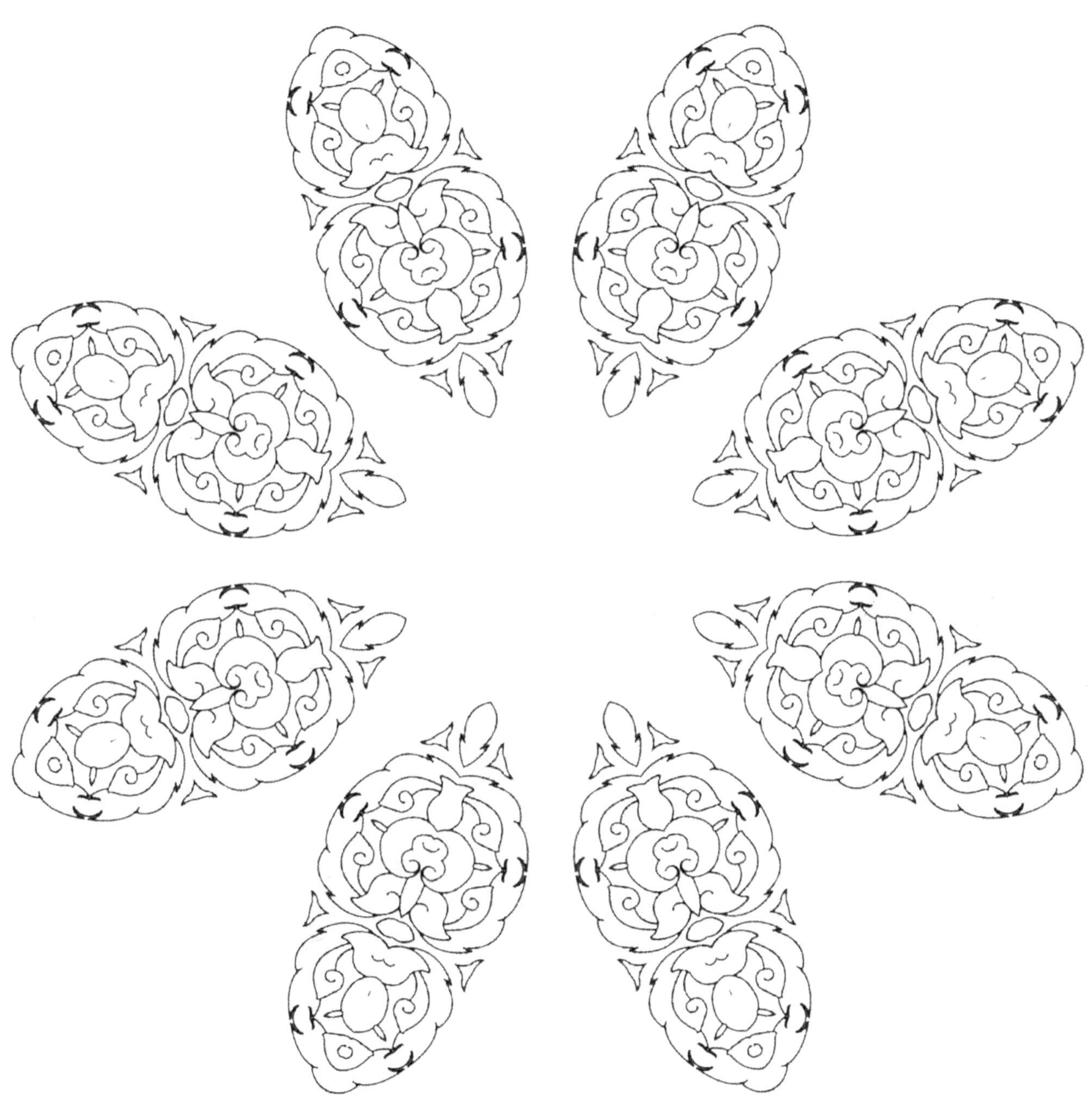

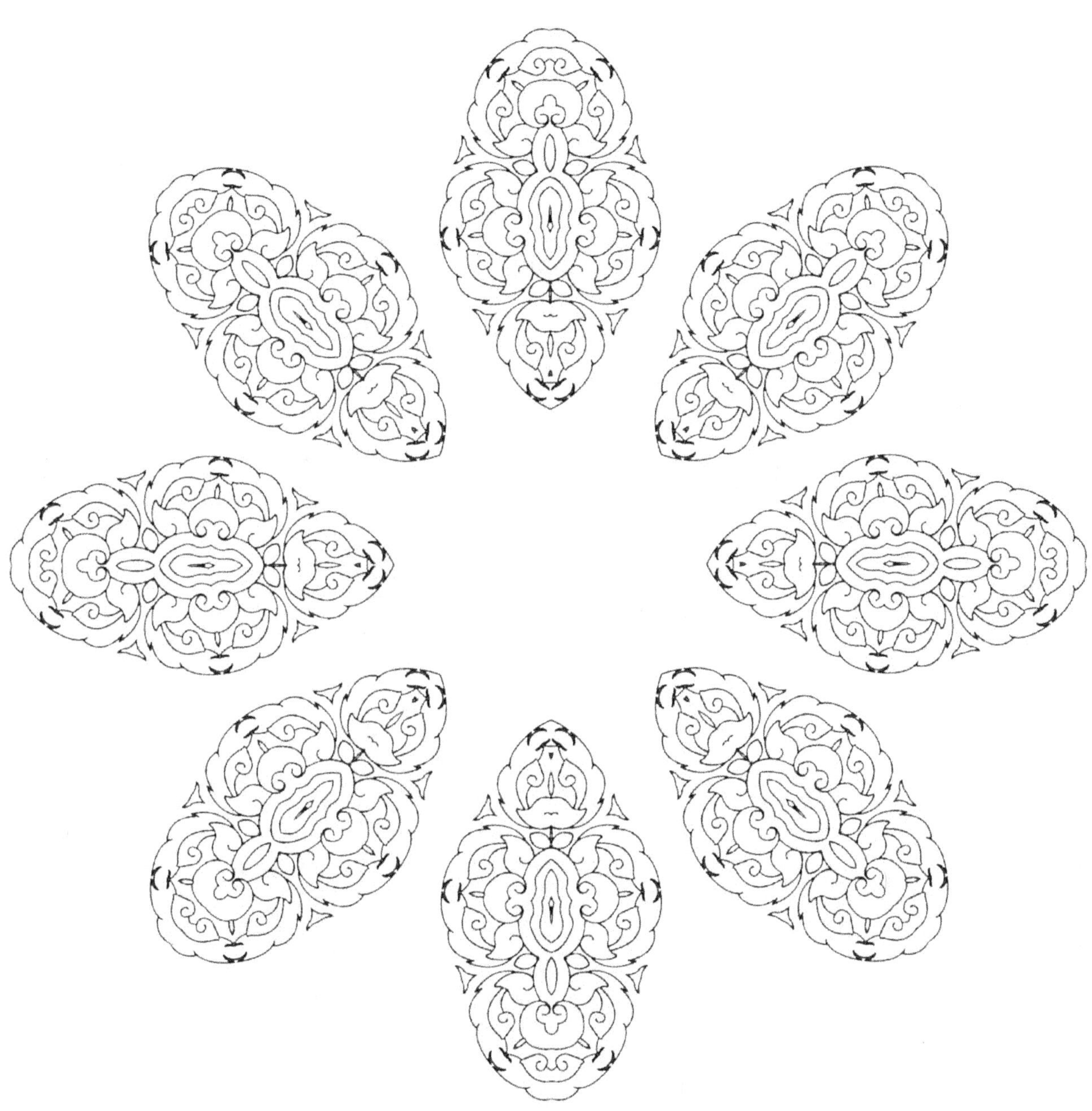

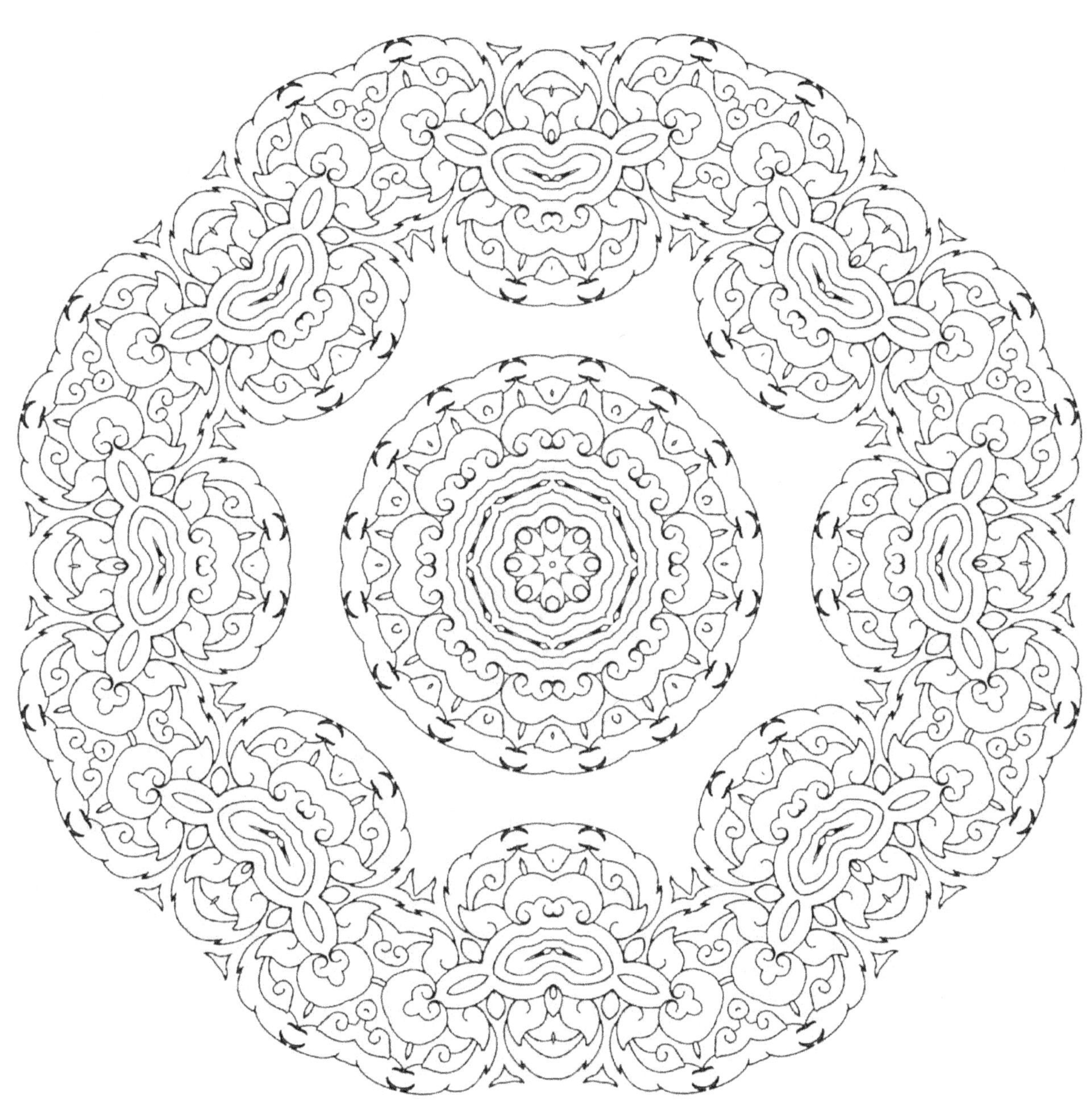

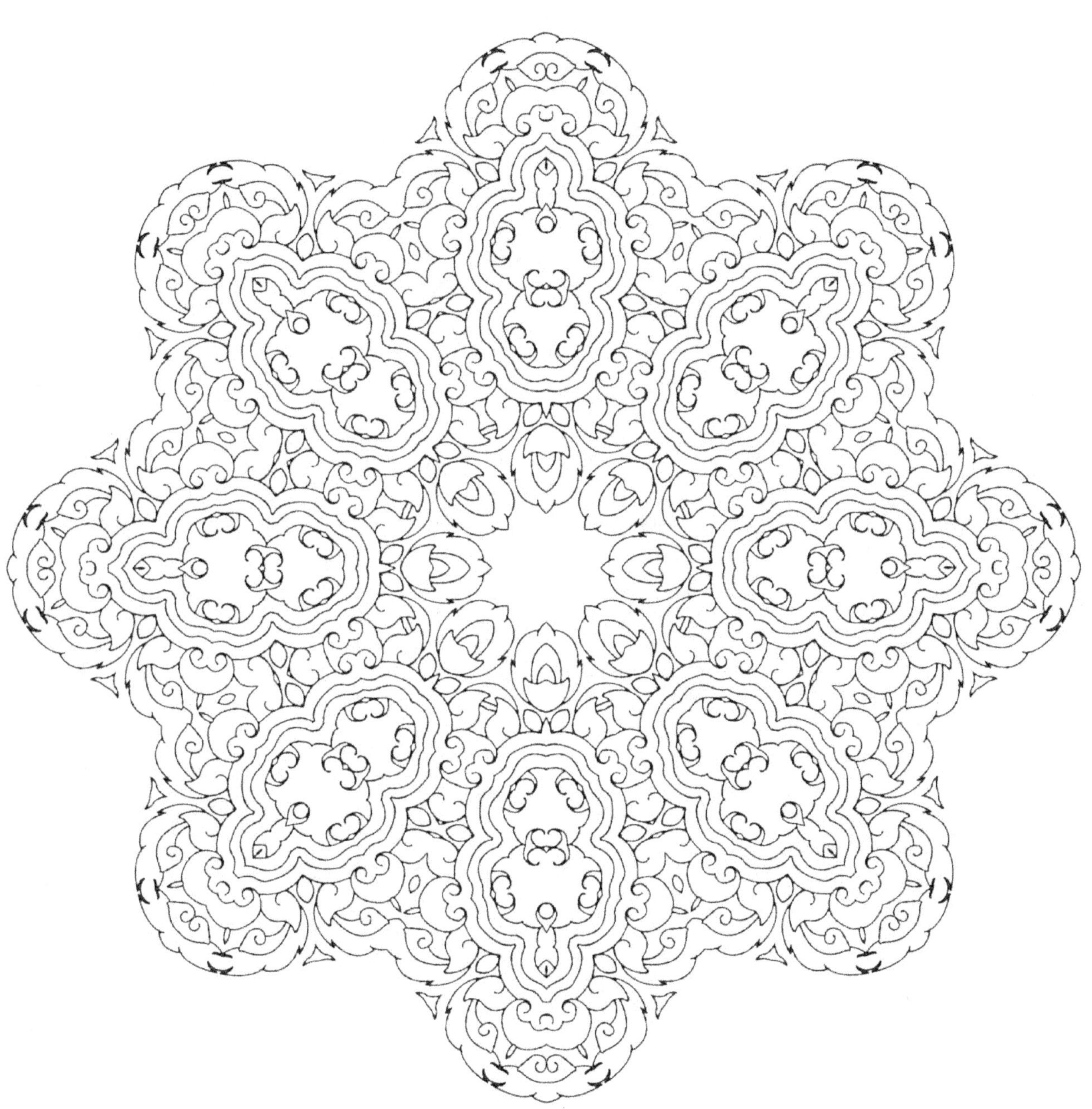

Thank you

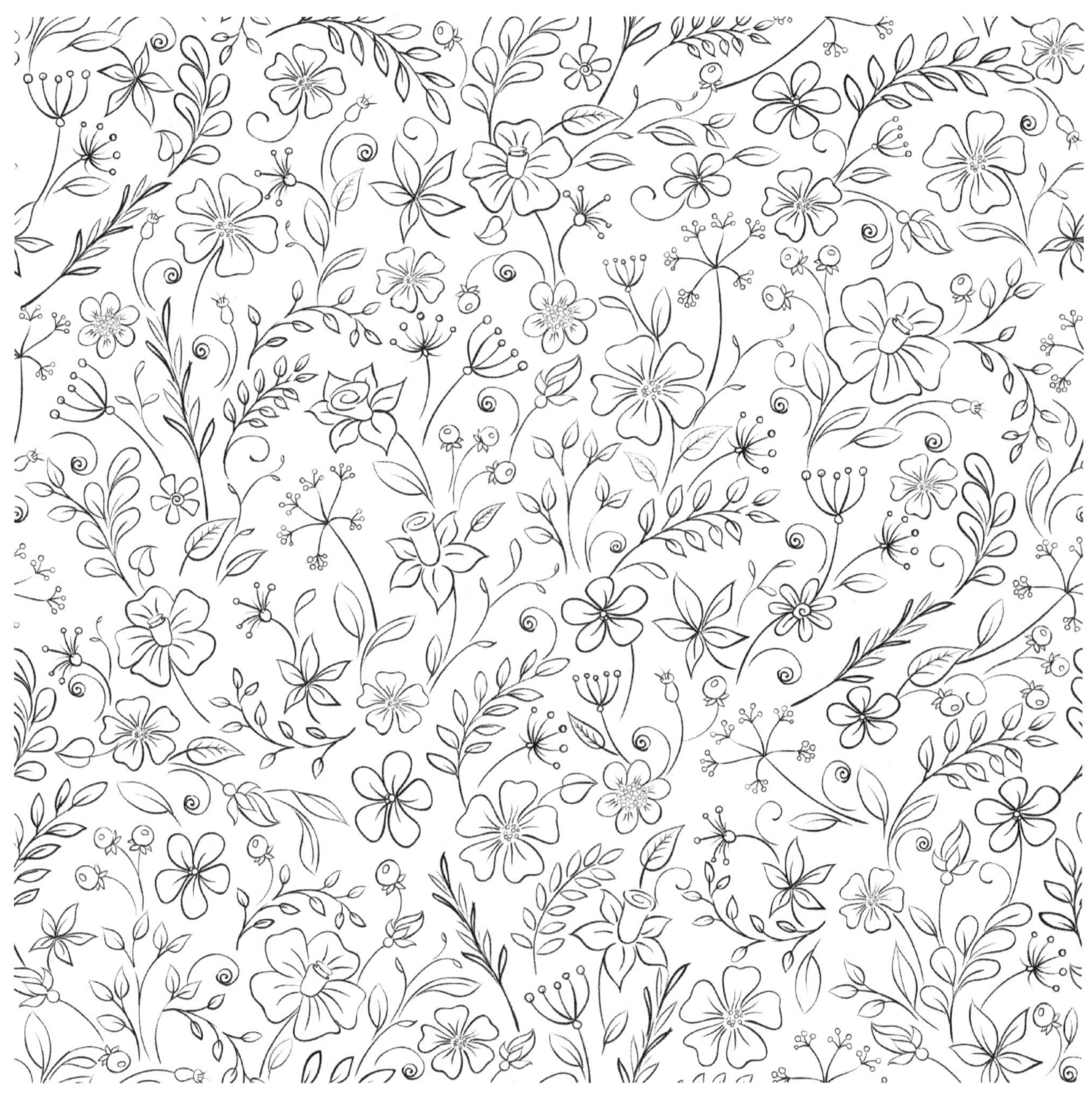